Sherwood Anderson:
Dimensions of His Literary Art

Sherwood Anderson:
Dimensions of His Literary Art

———————

A Collection of Critical Essays

———————

Edited by
DAVID D. ANDERSON

MICHIGAN STATE UNIVERSITY PRESS

1976

★
 ★
 ★
  ★
   ★

To the Memory of

Sherwood Anderson

and to

Eleanor Copenhaver Anderson

Contents

DAVID D. ANDERSON   Introduction: Life, Not Death,   xi
Is the Great Adventure

WILLIAM V. MILLER   Portraits of the Artist: Ander-   1
son's Fictional Storytellers

RAY LEWIS WHITE   The Warmth of Desire: Sex in   25
Anderson's Novels

WALTER B. RIDEOUT   Talbot Whittingham and An-   43
derson: A Passage to *Wines-
burg, Ohio*

WELFORD DUNAWAY   Anderson and the Problem of   63
TAYLOR   Belonging

LINDA W. WAGNER   Sherwood, Stein, The Sentence,   78
and Grape Sugar and Oranges

MARTHA MULROY   Anderson's Theories on   93
CURRY   Writing Fiction

WILLIAM A. SUTTON   Anderson's Letters to Marietta   113
D. Finley Hahn: A Literary
Chronicle

DAVID D. ANDERSON   Anderson and Myth   121

Acknowledgments

For the privilege of editing this book I am deeply grateful to many people, some of whose influence goes back a quarter of a century: Emerson Shuck, Russel B. Nye, and Bernard Duffey, who encouraged my interest in Sherwood Anderson; William B. Thomas, with whom I have had many conversations about books, writing, and Sherwood Anderson; the contributors, all of them friends as well as colleagues; my wife, Pat, whose patience and understanding have no limits; Mrs. Eleanor Anderson, whose kindnesses are beyond measure; Toni Pienkowski, for her constant, capable assistance; and Lyle Blair and Jean Busfield of the Michigan State University Press, who made its publication possible.

David D. Anderson

Introduction:
Life, Not Death,
Is the Great Adventure

Nearly fifteen years ago I first commented on the paradoxical nature of the criticism that has been directed at Sherwood Anderson's works: for nearly a generation before that time, critical consensus relegated Anderson to a relatively minor place in American literary history, and yet critics not only found it impossible to ignore him but gave him a great deal more attention than many writers considered to be major.

Fifteen years later, thirty-five years after Anderson's death and a century after his birth, that paradox continues to be the reality among many critics, particularly among those from the East (not too long ago, for example, Susan Sontag made the unfortunate observation that Anderson was so bad as to be almost laughable). However, during those fifteen years a number of things have happened to re-emphasize and re-shape the paradoxical in Anderson criticism. Anderson has been rediscovered by the anthologists to the point where no literary anthology, literary history, or freshman reader is complete without a selection from Anderson's works and commentary about him. Further, during those years a small group of critical admirers, most of whom had also known Anderson's countryside and his people, has grown to a sizable number; none is a critical apologist, but all, in subjecting Anderson's work to the most penetrating critical analysis, have learned much, disseminated a great deal of information, and given many interpretations, all of which combine to threaten or even demolish that paradox in this, Anderson's centennial year.

Perhaps the most important discovery that these newer critics have made is that Anderson is not a one-significant-book writer, nor does his literary reputation rest only upon a handful of short stories. Although *Winesburg, Ohio* is certainly his most important work, a first-rate work of literary art as well as a germinal book in the development of modern American literature, the list of Anderson's other accomplishments, in literary terms as well as in perceptive interpretations of America in flux, is one of the most impressive in our literary history.

From Anderson's early years, those which saw *Winesburg, Ohio* become a modern classic, critics have increasingly pointed out the importance of *Poor White,* certainly the most significant attempt to chronicle the impact of industrialism upon the Midwestern countryside and to tap the wellsprings of the American character in a tradition that goes back to Twain, Whitman, Emerson, and beyond. Perhaps equally important in this work, and largely ignored by Anderson's contemporaries as well as others who relegated him to the list of America's minor writers, is his treatment of women as human beings of great potential, skill, and insight, a characteristic that was to continue in his works, especially in those of the 1930s that have been unfortunately overlooked or ignored for so long.

During those early years, too, one must acknowledge the importance of two collections of short stories, *The Triumph of the Egg* and *Horses and Men,* not merely for some of the individual stories that they contain, as the earlier critics insisted, but because of the remarkable unity inherent in each volume, a unity that approximates that in *Winesburg, Ohio.* Although much of the longer fiction of these years—*Windy McPherson's Son, Marching Men,* and *Many Marriages*—is often less even, nevertheless each is a substantial addition to the literature of the individual's search for freedom and fulfillment in our age, and *Dark Laughter* is greatly superior to the others, so much so that it certainly deserves the status of the best seller that it nearly became.

Unfortunately denigrated and ignored by Anderson's contemporaries and successors in the twenty years after his death are the autobiographical documents—*A Story Teller's Story* and *Tar: A Midwest Childhood,* in particular—that are now seen, not as occasional pieces or repetitions, but as the careful examinations and continued reinterpretations of experience that they are—Anderson's own, but America's too.

At this point critical legend has insisted that Anderson's work had become redundant, tedious, and repetitious, best forgotten by those inclined to literary charity, but perhaps the most important contribution of the new Anderson critics has been the demolishing of that legend, one of the key elements in the first part of the paradox. The works from the late 1920s and early 1930s, it is now fortunately evident, are those of Anderson's maturity, perceptive and substantial interpretations of some of the many faces of America, past and present, in repose and in crisis. *Hello Towns!, Perhaps Women, No Swank,* and *Puzzled America* are not only the best of Anderson's journalism, that of the years during which he explored the grassroots of western Virginia and the back roads of America, but they are among the best American journalism, perceptive human documents, that are, in style and structure as well as in insight, worthy successors to *Winesburg, Ohio,* and as firmly rooted in the American experience as their better known predecessor.

Remarkably, it is now evident that during these last years Anderson's creative impulse, again contrary to legend, was strong. The two contemporary novels, *Beyond Desire* and *Kit Brandon,* and the collection of short stories, *Death in the Woods,* are substantial works, the latter containing two of the finest short stories in any language; and all of them, together with much of the journalism, continue the interpretation and examination not only of the American experience but of the American woman as human being, a course that Anderson had begun so significantly and successfully in *Poor White* more than a decade before.

During Anderson's last years he added a clear new dimension to his work, a dimension that is particularly eloquent in three works of varying lengths but all curiously alike, and each of them a substantial addition to Anderson's canon and the history of American literature in our time. These works were *The American County Fair, Home Town,* and his *Memoirs,* uncompleted at his death and, in its edited forms, still an imperfect work. In these three works Anderson continues and completes what he had tentatively attempted in his two volumes of verse, *Mid-American Chants* and *A New Testament:* he celebrates life itself, that which, in spite of its torments and frustrations, is, in its moments of fulfillment and sometimes even in spite of them, the supreme value that man can hold and the greatest good he can find.

In spite of the hostility of those critics who deny Anderson his profundity and even sometimes the essence of his humanity, this final celebration, this ultimate statement of meaning, is both profound and universal, and, as the new generation of Anderson's critics have learned, it is perhaps the most thoroughly documented statement of faith in all of American literary history—documented through the essence of Anderson's life and of American life in his time, both of which combine in the substance of his works. His achievement is neither fleeting nor insignificant, as the new young critics who have discovered him are well aware; his place in American literary history and in the affections of the growing numbers of his readers has continued to grow; and, as I commented nearly a decade ago, "as a man who approached life with reverence, who spoke of it with love, and who provided some of the most eloquent expressions of both in his time, his place is secure."

As we commemorate the one hundredth anniversary of his birth, not only is his place secure, but as the relevance of his works to contemporary America becomes increasingly evident, that role continues to grow, and the paradox apparent in Anderson criticism for so long diminishes accordingly, until, it is safe to predict, the early years of Anderson's second century will see it disappear entirely, together with the mistaken attempts at categorization—primitivist, naturalist, realist, among others—that have in recent years been demonstrated to be as mistaken as the continuing assertion that *Winesburg, Ohio,* his best work, was, in effect, his only work.

No better evidence exists to refute those who would minimize or deny Anderson's contribution to American literature than this collection of critical essays, some by authors whose names have been associated with Anderson criticism for a generation and others who have come to know him more recently, but all of whom contribute to giving Anderson the creative credit that has been denied him by so many for so long. As wide as the essays range in subject matter, they by no means exhaust all its potential, although they point out the direction that much of the criticism will take in Anderson's second century. At the same time these perceptive critics join me in this volume in confidently proclaiming not the end of Anderson's first century but the beginning of the second, that in which the paradox will vanish in the recognition that the substantial body of his work is a significant and permanent contribution to American literature and to our understanding of ourselves, our time, and our country, and whatever it is that gives them meaning and direction.

DAVID D. ANDERSON

Portraits of the Artist: Anderson's Fictional Storytellers

WILLIAM V. MILLER

Salient in the criticism of Sherwood Anderson's short fiction are issues of theme and form. These are proper emphases, for like Hawthorne's "iron-rod" unifying themes, Anderson's stories include shafts of his vision to which the other story elements adhere, and his heroic struggle for fictional form is evident not only in the fiction but also in the impact of his statements and example on the development of the modern short story. But with the possible exception of studies of the *Winesburg* grotesques, perhaps insufficient attention has been focused on Anderson's characterization: how he created characters and what character types emerge in the full range of his stories. For the characters are front center in the stories, many of which are chiefly fine vignettes, and in Anderson's theoretical statements he consistently stressed the importance of character creation.

The most important character type in the stories in frequency of appearance and fullness of presentation is the artist. But before examining this type, the central concern of

1

this study, some account should be made of the nature of Anderson's characterization and of the other character types that appear in the stories, though the scope of this essay permits only a summary treatment of these topics.[1]

I

Anderson plainly declared in "A Note on Realism" and elsewhere that the definitive source of his art was not the "real" world but the life of fancy: "What never seems to come quite clear is the simple fact that art is art. It is not life."[2] The imagination must constantly "feed" upon the world of reality, but in the artist's imagination the donnée loses much of its original character. Apparently Anderson gathered many impressions of people—viewed close at hand and at a distance—which lay, to use his persistent metaphor, like seeds in his imagination; but when characters appear on the written page, they have been remolded into the types we will be considering below. In a letter to his son John, Anderson described the ingathering: "Stories do not come to me as definite facts. I remember once being on a train, in a day coach, and seeing a man run across the field. The gesture stayed with me and resulted years afterward in a story call 'The Untold Lie' in Winesburg [sic]. This is one of many such experiences."[3]

Especially in the 1930s Anderson sought greater objectivity in his storytelling in *Kit Brandon* and "Nice Girl";[4] but his best work came, if it came at all, from his independent creative imagination which respected neither the integrity of the donnée nor the *intellectual* coercion of the author. Within his imagination his various experiences tended to cluster about a few dominant, emotionally charged experiences in his life; and thus the characters that are figured forth in the stories have predictable, repetitive traits. His treatment of Twain and Lincoln illustrates this tendency even in writing biography. As Jon S. Lawry has pointed out, Ander-

2

son's rather distorted view of Lincoln in the fragment *Father Abraham* is an instance of "the possessive impelling of the artist's own experience and intuition upon an object";[5] and Anderson clearly restyled Mark Twain's career to reflect his own struggles. Also, the characters, each with his own story, apparently came to Anderson as a kind of gift. As he wrote in his *Memoirs,* "the short story is the result of a sudden passion. It is an idea grasped whole as one would pick an apple in our orchard."[6]

As many commentators have noted, two of the most remarkable aspects of Anderson's stories are the narrative voice and what has been called their lyrical structures. Anderson employs dramatic monologue as in, for example, "I'm a Fool" and "I Want to Know Why"; but more often the narrative source is an informal storyteller who may be recalling events in which he was usually a minor participant or the self-conscious, omniscient narrator as in *Winesburg.* Whatever the exact relationship between the narrator and his materials may be—and we should be cautioned not to identify the speakers with Anderson even in the most autobiographical sketches—these narrators often characterize directly and further control reader responses by tones of compassion and the tacit invitation to share in the groping for the essence of a character.

This groping approach is a key to Anderson's fictional technique as Sister M. Joselyn has pointed out.

> The halting, tentative, digressive style, and the circular hovering or "Chinese box" approach to what happened thus do not so much demonstrate Anderson's affectation of the manner of oral story telling as they illustrate his understanding that the "epic" base of the story must be manipulated in such a way that weight is thrown upon the significance of the happenings as it reveals itself to the central consciousness and to the reader, rather than upon the events themselves. This is, of course, essentially a "poetic" strategy.[7]

3

What Anderson found significant was the expression of the essence of a character. In discussing the typical design of the *Winesburg* stories, Waldo Frank underscored this character emphasis and perceptively described the typical pattern of many of Anderson's stories:

> The "Winesburg" design is quite uniform: a theme-statement of a character with his mood, followed by a recounting of actions that are merely variations on the theme. These variations make incarnate what has already been revealed to the reader; they weave the theme into life by the always subordinate confrontation of other characters (usually one) and by an evocation of landscape and village.[8]

As we look more closely at the tales, we perceive that because his characters exist primarily through their interior lives, the reader is given only characteristic gestures, and a paucity of physical details; that brief, striking actions function as "epiphanies," illuminated images that fix the character as well as the theme in the reader's mind—frustrated Alice Hindman running naked in the rain, the scene in the "rummy-looking farmhouse" viewed by the adolescent who wants to know why; and that setting details often serve symbolically to reveal character further as in the description of the isolated office of the lonely Dr. Reefy in "Paper Pills," or in the same story the misshapen but sweet apples that are emblems of Reefy's character.

Lionel Trilling noted the limitations of Anderson's characterization by observing accurately that "we do not love people for their essence or their souls, but for their having a certain body, or wit, or idiom, certain specific relationships with things and other people, and for a dependable continuity of existence: we love them for being there."[9] Anderson's characterization *is* circumscribed, but Frederick Hoffman has offered qualification and the proper context for evaluating this aspect of Anderson's art: "Anderson's characters are

4

real, but in a peculiar sense; they become real to us only if
and when we suspend ordinary judgment and accept them—
not for what they appear—but for what they think and
feel."[10] We find in Anderson's characterization neither range
nor the full texture of personality that Trilling describes, but
the incarnation of a few intensely felt and memorable in-
sights into human personality.

II

One may rather arbitrarily but usefully classify the drama-
tis personae of all of the published short stories into seven
major groups: grotesques, businessmen, professionals, mountaineers, women, adolescents, and artists. An examination of
these types permits one both to isolate and understand Anderson's compelling interests and to gain insight into the
characters of individual stories. We will want to see what
qualities of character Anderson's imagination had an affinity
for as well as what social types touched him most deeply and
perhaps why.

Unlike these other categories the grotesques do not consti-
tute a distinctive societal role. But, of course, they are definitively presented in *Winesburg;* and the grotesque syndrome
appears, though less poignantly, in many other characters. In
the most searching analysis to date of the concept of grotesqueness, Ralph Ciancio has explored the social, sexual,
and mythic roots of the grotesques as a basis for asserting
that for Anderson grotesqueness "was nothing more than a
metaphor of the natural condition of man . . . of his compul-
sive hearkening to the infinite call of transcendence which
finitude makes impossible from the start."[11] His study rein-
forces my view that Anderson's most persistent theme is the
often futile struggle of human beings for transcendence
which in those rare moments when it is achieved is associated
with beauty and order. The grotesqueness found in various
degrees in his protagonists distinguishes these characters

from philistines (e.g., Tom Willard) on the one hand and the *much* rarer and never fully realized artists on the other. We may profitably keep the grotesque pattern in mind as we consider the other roles.

The most frequent objects of contempt in Anderson's stories are businessmen. This is not surprising for a writer whose career was styled by the mythologized gesture of repudiating the business world, the metamorphosis of the "Roof-Fix" businessman into the Bohemian artist. And the fact that most of his fictional attacks on advertising men came later in his career, in the 1930s, was partially explained by his observation to Charles Bockler in 1933 that earlier he "had too much hatred."[12] Anderson's implicit indictment of businessmen was that they murder life—their own lives and the lives of artists. In "Brother Death" it is clear that John Gray and his son paid too high a price for money and power. In analyzing the submission of the boy to his father's will Anderson asserts, through the narration, "Something in you must die before you can possess and command."[13] The businessman directly destroys artists through vicious practices, as in "Blackfoot's Masterpiece"; or more often characters prostitute their talents, as in "Milk Bottles," "A Chicago Hamlet," "I Get So I Can't Go On," and "Off Balance."

Featured characters in sixteen stories are professional men —seven doctors, three lawyers, five professors, and one architect. Anderson was always somewhat awed by educated people. He admired and wooed such Eastern intellectuals as Waldo Frank, Paul Rosenfeld, and Van Wyck Brooks; and each of his marriages was to a woman who represented for him a disciplined culture he found wanting in his own background. Although he respects his professional characters, especially the doctors, most of them have buried lives that often contrast with their public lives, and some of them have severe communication problems.

Both of the Winesburg doctors should be sued for malpractice, but both are philosophers and writers. Parcival prefers warning George and writing his book, the thesis of which is "that everyone in the world is Christ and they are all crucified,"[14] to treating the few patients he has. Reefy is likewise slovenly, careless, and "unprofessional" in his public acts; but the sweetness of his character is revealed to the two women in his life and in the fine, poetic thoughts expressed but not communicated on the paper pills. Three other doctors are superior to Parcival and Reefy professionally (although Anderson offers very few details of their professional acts), but all three have hidden lives that they never successfully express. Lester Cochran ("Unlighted Lamps") was loved by his wife and daughter as well as by his patients, but his silence drives his wife away, and he dies before he can express his love for his daughter. The doctor in "A Moonlight Walk" is paralyzed when he attempts to write, despite his fluency as an oral storyteller. In "Pastoral" the active, perceptive life of the overtly taciturn, boorish doctor is revealed in love letters he wrote but did not send to a plain woman clerk. The one lawyer that Anderson portrayed with any depth, John Wilkins in "A Dead Dog," does not write, but like these doctors his public style as an implacable prosecuting attorney contrasts with the deep sensitivity hidden beneath his brusque manner.

Through three of the college professors Anderson offers further observation about his own craft. The historian in "The Man in the Brown Coat" and the professor in "The Flood" are living examples of the limitations of strictly intellectual communication. Despite their achievements in writing academic prose, both are victims of their feelings: the historian's wife is a stranger to him, and the professor discovers the inadequacy of intellectual values against the flood tides of emotions. Among these professors, only the protagonist in "In a Strange Town" has found a way to social and psychic wholeness. Periodically, he renews himself by visiting strange towns where he observes strange people and writes about them. He is there to lose himself and to exercise his fancy—a therapy Anderson endorsed in his speech, "A Writer's Conception of Realism."

7

From 1926 to 1937 Anderson wrote a distinctive group of thirteen stories set in Appalachia, especially the environs of his last permanent home near Marion, Virginia. Two central motives inform Anderson's characterization of the mountaineers in these stories: a strong desire to cut through the fog of romance surrounding mountaineers in order to reveal their essential stubborn courage and pride and greater attention to frustrations less psychological than products of ignorance and poverty. Joe in "A Sentimental Journey" epitomizes Anderson's mountain people who, typically, are unsophisticated primitives who love their land and struggle heroically to maintain their integrity. Joe is moved by poverty and curiosity to seek work in a mining town far from his mountain home, wife, and thirteen children. However, when the sounds and black ugliness of the factory become overwhelming, he and his seven-year-old son travel three days and nights through bitter cold and snowdrifts to reach the white snow and quiet of their mountain home. In addition to Joe, Anderson respects all of these hill people for asserting their humanity in a society circumscribed by poverty and ignorance: Tom Halsey ("A Mountain Marriage") who assaults a rich customer twice his size to get money to save his dying wife; Poly Grubb ("A Mountain Dance") who dances, drinks, and fornicates all night but will not leave his aged parents while they are alive; the young pregnant girl ("These Mountaineers") who tells the narrator to go to hell after he touches her pride by offering her money.

Both women and adolescent boys are character groups deserving much fuller consideration than can be offered here. The women characters are properly approached through Anderson's biography, through a consideration of his four marriages and especially through his idealized mother Emma Anderson, who is apotheosized in "Death in the Woods." This evidence and his own statements, despite a few comments such as "The women are a hundred times as good as we men,"[15] lead one to conclude that his true persuasion was that women are qualitatively different from men and lower in his esteem. A revealing statement appears in an unpublished memoir: "I would have gone all on some fool's track with her for I have seldom been a wholehearted lover of women. I could never believe in women artists and cannot to this day. Perhaps in some essential part of me—never in the flesh—I have all of my life, loved men more than I have ever loved women."[16] The most common roles of his women characters reflect his often idealized stereotyping of womankind—they are managers, defenders of the home who entrap men, wholehearted givers to men, frustrated gropers after a higher life, or combinations of these types. A few examples will serve to suggest the patterns of each of these feminine roles.

A frequent motif in a number of stories is the relationship between a bemused, confused man and a capable, resourceful woman. In "Another Wife" a middle-aged couple apparently blunder into an understanding that they will marry. The widower doctor is unsure and bewildered by his wife's "modernity," but she is understanding, patient, and sure of what she wants. Other managers include Aunt Sally in "A Meeting South"; Gretchen, the nurse, in "The Rabbit-Pen"; the doctor's wife in "Pastoral"; the girl in "Nice Girl"; and the mother in "The Egg." In the latter story, the father wants to "rise"; but the mother is, as the narrator states, "incurably ambitious" for the family, determining most of the family moves including decisions such as having a restaurant, renting a store building, and keeping the restaurant open at night.

In "The Contract" appears the powerful image of the feelings of a young man as he confronts the necessity of getting married: "He felt like a beast who in playing about at night in the forest has suddenly put his foot into a trap."[17] Anderson's indictment of marriage can be even stronger (e.g., "Brothers"); however, he could also be sympathetic with the necessity for marriage in our culture. The best dramatization of this marriage dilemma is "The Untold Lie" in *Winesburg,* where the concentration is not on Ray's wife who wants him to "hustle" but upon what Ray should tell young Winters about marriage. Despite all his training, Ray runs to tell Winters not to be trapped into marriage; but he does not, for he realized that "whatever I told him would be a lie" (p. 209).

In the characterization of some of his women as "feeders," Anderson expressed his guilt about the exploitation of women by himself and other men. The women in "Death in the Woods" epitomize this "feeding," about which Anderson wrote in 1937: "It seems to me that the theme of the story is the persistent animal hunger of men. There are these women who spend their whole lives, rather dumbly, feeding this hunger."[18] In one short paragraph in the story, forms of the word "feed" are used five times. This guilt (with haunting memories of his mother in the background) mingles with admiration for the feeding women in such stories as "Not Sixteen," "Daughters," "Like a Queen," "White Spot," "The Teacher," and "The Man's Story." Anderson's artist-writers particularly need this selfless love to sustain their art; Kate Swift and Elizabeth Willard are but two of his characters who passionately nurture incipient and accomplished artists.

A final grouping includes perhaps his most successful women characters, those intensely alive, sensitive seekers after a higher degree of fulfillment like Elizabeth Willard, Kate Swift, Elsie Leander ("The New Englander"), May Edgley ("Unused"), Mary Cochran ("Unlighted Lamps"), and Rosalind Wescott ("Out of Nowhere into Nothing"). All of these women have Elizabeth's need: "Like all the women in the world, she wanted a real lover" (p. 224); and some seek fulfillment through sex. But all of them are frustrated—to some degree by the failures of men and hypocritical moral codes as Rex Burbank has suggested[19]—however, the hypothetical "real lover" is needed by both sexes, one with whom there is sustained, patient, shared understanding of and respect for one's essential aloneness. Kate Swift is a "feeder," but more definitively the real Kate is "the most eagerly passionate soul" in Winesburg. And each of these other women maintains a buried life that is tragically unnourished by society.

In addition to stories featuring George Willard five other of Anderson's best stories have adolescent boys as protagonists: "I'm a Fool," "The Man Who Became a Woman," "I Want to Know Why," "The Sad Horn Blowers," and "An Ohio Pagan."[20] All of these stories, which were published between 1919 and 1923, reveal Mark Twain's influence and draw heavily with rich detail on Anderson's youth in Clyde, Ohio, which he left in 1896, the year after his mother died. The pattern of each youth's development is basically the same.

Each youth is at first naive and innocent, responding ingenuously and joyfully to his environment. Typically, a measure of the protagonist's character in "I Want to Know Why" is the intense pleasure he gets from racetrack sights, sounds, and odors; and even the speaker in "I'm a Fool," whose intellectual grasp of his situation bodes ill for someone nineteen years old, glories in nature.

Then something happens to each boy; and, like Will Appleton ("The Sad Horn Blowers"), each is "swinging in space" (p. 116), his private world of value deflected from its orbit. One must not oversimplify. The boys are unique; they function in unique contexts; and the time of crisis may be a culmination of a series of dislocating acts, one intense moment, or but the beginning moment in a period of adjustment. The deaths of their mothers are watershed events for both Will and George Willard, but Will's loss of home becomes palpable only after his sister announces her marriage, and George has served a long apprenticeship in human behavior before Elizabeth dies. Herman Dudley experiences a long nightmarish experience; torn between "track" and middle-class values, the speaker in "I'm a Fool" lies himself into unhappiness; and the youngest of these characters (fifteen) in "I Want to Know Why" and Tom in "An Ohio Pagan" are shaken by acts they witness.

11

The best measure of each adolescent's distinctiveness is how he responds to his crisis. Three are left in varied degrees of confusion. Irving Howe is right in his view that "I'm a Fool" is inferior in complexity of experience to other tales including "I Want to Know Why" and "The Man Who Became a Woman," but considered in the comic tradition the boy's muddled social values provide more charm and poignance than Howe would grant.[21] The youth in "I Want to Know Why" is more fully realized because of the consistency of his reaction to the scene in the "rummy farmhouse" with his dramatized sensitive nature, and also because his encounter with the paradoxes of the commingling of beauty and ugliness, good and evil, touches universal chords in all of us. Even more effective is the presentation of Herman Dudley's "initiation" experience, for not only are the scenes in which he moves toward sexual confirmation powerful but also the addition of the older Dudley's adult sentience adds resonance and perceptiveness to the story.

George Willard, Tom Edwards, and Will Appleton all come through the adolescent crisis with a new sense of direction. Since Tom's story was conceived as a part of a longer work,[22] Anderson is concerned in Tom's development less with any clash of values than with the gradual development of his awareness; but at the close Tom leaves for the city, committed to the tasks of earning beauty and a woman through formal education. Will Appleton has George's deep sense of aloneness after Kate's letter cuts the last home tie; however he, too, finds through the old cornet player that necessary adjustment to adulthood George made with Helen's aid. Will discovers that all men are lost children in the universe, but "if one were a child and lost in a vast, empty space, one could at least talk to some other child. One could have conversations, understand perhaps something of the eternal childishness of oneself and others" (p. 117).

We notice in the characterization of these adolescents how highly Anderson valued the idealism of the young. Even in a world hostile to beauty, one must retain a measure of hope

12

and ingenuous receptiveness to beauty. These lessons of adolescence learned only intuitively by the young men await confirmation by the mature artists.

III

The most important character type in Anderson's stories is the artist. His stories are filled not only with painters and writers but also with potential artists, storytellers like May Edgley in "Unused"; and what may be called the "artistic impulse" is shared by an even wider scope of characters. Then, of course, the distinctive narrators, whether they be Anderson thinly disguised or separate characters, are actively present in the stories, apparently creating the tale as it progresses and inviting attention to the process through little asides like "I don't know how I learned this" or "you know how it is." Indeed, after we recognize the full dimensions of the role of the artist in Anderson's fiction, rare is the story in which we do not discover elements of this role.

The impulse that Anderson declared was behind his own decision to become a writer one finds in many of his protagonists. "I presume that we all who begin the practice of an art begin out of a great hunger for order. We want brought into consciousness something that is always there but that gets so terribly lost."[23] This "something" is a sense of beauty which Anderson once said was "the most vital thing to men."[24] Even the prosaic Ray Pearson in "The Untold Lie" is powerfully moved by the natural beauty around him. "The beauty of the country about Winesburg was too much for Ray on that fall evening. . . . Of a sudden he forgot all about being a quiet farm hand and throwing off the torn overcoat began to run across the field. As he ran he shouted a protest against his life, against all life, against everything that makes life ugly" (p. 207).

While other motives also operate, this desire to express a perceived order is a force within many of Anderson's ama-

13

teur storytellers such as May Edgely, Tom Hunt in "A Dead Dog," Tom in "A Chicago Hamlet," Luther Ford in "A Jury Case," and Helen in "When They Got Married." In addition to the sheer joy of telling stories shared by all of these amateurs, May finds in her created world of lies a sanctuary from her predatory community. In "A Chicago Hamlet," Tom is compelled to tell stories by an inner necessity much like that process Anderson described in reference to his own art: "When a story had attained form [in Tom's imagination] it had to be told about every so often."[25]

Furthermore, Anderson insisted that "the artist is after all but the craftsman working more intensely in more complex and delicate materials."[26] And he rejected the romantic notion that the artist is a special kind of human being. In one unpublished story, "Brother Earl," Earl's brother John, another crass businessman, dehumanizes Earl by stressing his "artistic impulses." John's simple but well-meaning wife offers to pose in the nude for Earl, but Earl thinks she wants him as a lover. When he discovers that her motives are kindly but not erotic, he is violently repelled by a relationship that denied his natural feelings.

Nevertheless, Anderson's conception of the artist in the stories is more specifically delineated, including the artist's distinguishing characteristics, dangers to which he is vulnerable, and social problems the artist encounters. Among the artist's characteristics are capacity for growth, talent with and respect for language, involvement yet detachment, an especially active imagination, idealism without romanticism, courage, and honesty.

Of course, the only extended study of the artist's development among the works considered here is in *Winesburg*, a work which Edwin Fussell regarded as "a *Bildungsroman* of a rather familiar type, the 'portrait of the artist as a young man,' in a period immediately preceding his final discovery of métier."[27] Fussell argues cogently that George's development illustrates Anderson's view "that the artist's essential quality must be defined as a capacity for growth which he

14

refuses to attribute to any of the grotesques."[28] To be sure, George is only a potential artist; and, since most of Anderson's fictional artists are not dynamic, this trait is illustrated only indirectly in stories other than the *Winesburg* sequence. We may recall that Herman Dudley admires the writer Tom Means but expresses doubts about whether Means ever achieved his goal of writing "the way a well-bred runs or trots or paces" (p. 60). It is consistent with the story's theme to suggest that Means may have failed as a writer because he failed to grow in his understanding beyond the naive idealism which he expressed so well for the youth. We should also keep in mind the impetus toward growth at least implicit in the basic drive for fulfillment in so many of Anderson's characters—not only artists but also the adolescents, the women, and the professionals.

Talent with language is not enough. The artist must respect language and the motives behind expression. In "Two Lovers" our sympathies are with John who speaks haltingly but sincerely, not with the advertising executive who describes his loves beautifully. The narrator in "The Triumph of the Modern" becomes intoxicated with words, but profanes his gift to exploit an aunt's sympathy. As Glen A. Love and others have pointed out, a vital part of George Willard's apprenticeship is learning to use language wisely.[29] He loves to express himself: "The desire to say words overcame him and he said words without meaning, rolling them over on his tongue and saying them because they were brave words, full of meaning. 'Death,' he muttered, 'night, the sea, fear, loveliness' " (p. 185). But in "An Awakening," from which this quotation is taken, all of his words are impotent, contrasting with the silent, purposive actions of Ed Handby. And George learns the lessons of active listening and finally how inadequate speech can be during the climactic scene in "Sophistication," as he and Helen wordlessly share their aloneness. To an aspiring writer Anderson wrote, "Try to let life flow through you a little. Above all forget words for a long long time. Keep silent a lot. Don't even say too many words.

15

Remember that words are very tender little things and that these goddam people [a writer's school] have tricked you into an almost unforgivable rudeness with them."[30]

However, the artist must have talent. In "A Chicago Hamlet" Tom is full of stories, but he lacks the shaping verbal aptitude. Although the writer-narrator in "A Moonlight Walk" envies the doctor's rich experiences with people, he recognizes his own special gift. "There is, however, this consolation: the problem is never to find and know a little the people whose stories are interesting. There are too many stories. The great difficulty is to tell the stories" (p. 264). The orally eloquent doctor expresses the complaint of many would-be writers: "When I get my pen in hand, I become dumb" (p. 264).

In his society the artist must be deeply involved with people, yet detached. The protagonist of Anderson's first published story, "The Rabbit-Pen," writes popular novels but is incapable of significant human contact. His human failures are contrasted with the competencies of the maid and the stableman, both of whom grasp life cleanly and manage the others. George Willard serves an apprenticeship of empathy with the grotesques, and the professor-writer in "In a Strange Town" is psychologically recreated by going among strangers. Anderson stated the case for involvement in a letter to his son John: "Myself thinking later, as I walked how all such people [a woman writer refused the responsibility of learning to drive] do get out of the responsibility of entering into life in their work . . . also that the not taking responsibility was a kind of way to death . . ."[31]

The detachment of the artist is most strikingly illustrated by Edgar Wilson in "The Man's Story," who lives as often in the imaginative world as he does in the real world. He is oblivious to his flophouse apartment and indifferent when accused of murdering the woman he lived with. Most bizarrely, he continues in a poetic trance even while the woman walking beside him is shot. Through all this he writes poems about the walls that isolate us from one another. In examining George Willard's role, Fussell contended that "the view of the artist presented in *Winesburg* is "that of a man who joins sympathy and understanding to detachment and imperturbability."[32] The social ramifications of the artist's need sometimes to sever human relationships will be considered later.

As we might expect from the abundant biographical evidence, Anderson's artists have very active imaginative lives. William A. Sutton's interviews with Anderson's Elyria, Ohio, neighbors underscore the vital role Anderson assigned to the imagination. According to one witness Anderson played out imaginatively riotous scenes with his children, and on another occasion Cornelia explained to her puzzled stepmother that in playing with Robert, "Sherwood was training Robert's imagination."[33] In *A Story Teller's Story* and on other occasions Anderson expressed how intensely real the life of fancy was for him, the source of his creations and often a sanctuary from the ugly real world.

As has been noted, many of the fictional artists have rich imaginative lives, but perhaps the best accounts of these experiences appear in "A Part of Earth," the sketch in which Anderson described the creation of "Hands," and in "The Lost Novel." In the former he wrote, "As ever when I was drunk my imagination played wildly. With head awhirl I lay on my bed, staring through my window into the rainy street, and figures began appearing before my eyes" (p. 218). The writer in "The Lost Novel" has similar experiences: "In his fancy, figures are moving back and forth" (p. 143). "He said there were all sorts of characters and situations in his head" (p. 146).

An intense idealism, so admired in the adolescents, may also be a part of the artist's makeup. An extreme case is that of the handsome title figure in "Italian Poet in America," who self-destructively pursues an ideal woman who would love him and accept his love. After deserting the Italian girl he had married in New York and abusing another woman, he continues his quest in Chicago where he contracts syphillis and dies symbolically worshiping a prostitute in the snow before the whorehouse. But before he dies, the poet declares, "I have found the thing I have been seeking in her and she has found it in me."[34] In seeking his moments of magic Anderson constantly risks being ludicrous. Here I think he fails, but the questing urge is well epitomized. A scene in "White Spot" illustrates the more typical, deeper ideal relationship in which sexual expression is only a means to the ideal of beauty. The writer recalls lying with a woman in a cheap Chicago hotel:

> Now, for an hour, two, three hours, the puzzling lust of the flesh is gone. The mind, the fancy, is free.
> It must have been that fancy, the always busy imagination of the artist-man, she wanted.
> She began to speak softly of the white spot. "It floats in the darkness," she said softly, and I think I did understand, almost at once, her need . . .
> After the flesh the spirit. Minds, fancy, draw close now . . .
> It (the white spot) is the thing lost. It eludes us.
> It belongs to us. It is our whiteness (p. 262).

This passionate seeking after the ideal is not limited to artists: women create out of their bodies and other craftsmen share the aspiration. Nor is it an idealism that blinds the seeker from the often sordid reality. Every close reader of Anderson has noted his refusal to gloss over evil and sordidness. The writer in "White Spot" tells the woman she is beautiful as he leaves her, but the story ends with these words: "A lie. There was no beauty. The night, the street, the city" (p. 263). Nevertheless, idealism expressed in a persistent struggle toward a life of fuller realization found especially in creating beautiful forms remains an important trait of the artist-writer.

Anderson was extremely sensitive to the moral dimensions of the writer's creative acts. "I think this whole thing [a

18

writer's motives] must be in some way tied up with something I can find no other word to describe aside from the word 'morality.' I suppose I think that the author who doesn't struggle all his life to achieve this form, let it be form, betrays this morality. It is terribly important because to my way of thinking, this morality may be the only true morality there is in the world."[35] With Hemingway he shared an almost fanatical insistence upon the honesty and courage of a writer, fictional or real. In "Milk Bottles" Ed's creative writing has gone "sour" because the honesty of his approach to his work has been compromised by his immersion in the advertising world. The protagonist in "Blackfoot's Masterpiece" and Anderson himself in "A Part of Earth" need courage to deny their keen material desires for the sake of art. The virtue stressed in Anderson's affectionate vignette of Faulkner in "A Meeting South" is the fictionalized Faulkner's (David's) courage as he lived and wrote "in the black house of pain" (p. 175).

The pitfalls in an artist's career are latent in his general characteristics. The artist-writer is always vulnerable to the siren calls of a materialistic society, sought by those who need "word-slingers" to move the products of industrialism. Thus, Billy Moore in "Off-Balance," Ed in "Milk Bottles," and the copywriter in "I Get So I Can't Go On" have sullied their talents by selling out to business.

Because idealism too easily becomes romanticism, a writer's idealism may also betray him. As noted earlier, Anderson's characterizations of the mountaineers were partially Anderson's conscious reactions to the popular view of mountain people in the fiction of the 1920s. "People of the outside world think of these mountain people as underfed, illiterate and dangerous. They have been fed up with romances."[36] One of the best indexes of George Willard's immaturity is his artificial approach to writing a love story in "The Thinker," in which he declares to Seth Richmond that, as an apparent prelude to his writing the story, he was going to fall in love with Helen White. George's romantic view of writing is shared by Ed in "Milk Bottles" and by John in "Brother Earl," both of whom are targets for Anderson's satire.

From Anderson's point of view, the artistic temperament could be anathema to married life; but for the right woman artists may be "the only lovers" (p. 145). "The Lost Novel" is a valuable document for understanding both Anderson's life and his concept of the artist's role. In 1928, the year that story was published, Anderson's marriage with Elizabeth Prall was breaking up and his writing career was at a standstill. The satisfactions of editing the two Marion, Virginia, newspapers had waned. One of only three stories set in Europe (Anderson may have chosen a distant setting to disguise a very personal subject matter), "The Lost Novel" concerns the difficulties of a successful writer in writing his second novel and in reconciling art with family life. After he began to write, "He, *of course* [italics mine], neglected his job, his wife, his kids" (p. 145). As is the case in "The Yellow Gown," his wife is completely out of his consciousness while he writes; and when she interrupted while he was writing, he knocked her down. After she left him he is ashamed, but not repentent.

Despite the implications in "The Lost Novel" that the woman was not "pagan" enough for the writer, the problem is that both Anderson and his artist characters misuse women but find them indispensable. Anderson once wrote, "I've never been able to work without a woman to love. Perhaps I'm cruel. . . . I take from her. I know damn well I don't give enough."[37] This view is reflected in a number of stories but most specifically in "The Man's Story," in which the reader is asked to believe that the relationship between Wilson and the weakly developed woman was mutually satisfactory. Whatever he gives her to secure her extraordinary devotion, she helps him escape out of himself. The process is clear: by escaping from self he has gained psychic health; having achieved health he is able to communicate his experiences in poetry.

This survey of the major character types yields firm patterns of characterization which can illuminate individual stories. In the full reading context of such stories as "Death in The Woods" and "I Want to Know Why" are not only the biographical data so pertinent to Anderson's essentially lyrical art but also the repetitive images of Anderson's fictional women and adolescents. Even more ubiquitous is the motif of the artist's role, sometimes as a major theme but often muted in nuances of behavior. Although the range of his characterization is limited, it is intense and valuable; for if some insight is profound enough, its ramifications are infinite. That is why, for example, reading about each new, individual grotesque in *Winesburg* can be a fresh, moving experience.

William Faulkner's account of how Anderson's life style as a writer encouraged him in his career confirms but is only the tip of the iceberg of Anderson's pervasive influence among twentieth century fiction writers, though the definitive study of his influence has not been written. In thousands of letters, in speeches, in three full biographies, and now as we have seen in the full dimensions of the stories, Anderson gave a remarkably complete portrayal of the artist's role. Many of the facets of the artist's experiences as he perceived and articulated them are not unique. What is unique is the peculiar intensity of his commitment to the life of the imagination—the focal point of his deepest sense of morality—and the unusual degree in which the fictional portraits reflect Anderson's vision of the artist's role.

NOTES

1. For more detailed analyses of two character types, the women and the mountaineers, see my earlier studies: "Earth Mothers, Succubi, and Other Ectoplasmic Spirits: the Women in Sherwood Anderson's Short Stories," *Mid-America I* (Fall 1973): 64–81 and "In Defense of Mountaineers: Sherwood Anderson's Hill Stories," *Forum* 15, No. n (Spring 1974): 51–58. This study and the two earlier ones are based on a consideration

of *all* Anderson's published and a few unpublished stories.

2. *Sherwood Anderson's Notebook* (New York: Boni and Liveright, 1926), p. 72.

3. *Letters of Sherwood Anderson,* edited by Howard Mumford Jones and Walter B. Rideout (Boston: Little, Brown, 1953), p. 357. All *published* letters will be cited from this source, henceforth shortened to *Letters.*

4. Letter to Roger Sergel, *Letters,* p. 333.

5. " 'Death in the Woods' and the Artist's Self in Sherwood Anderson," *PMLA* 74 (1959): 310.

6. *Memoirs* (New York: Harcourt, Brace, 1942), p. 341. *Note:* This is the older *Memoirs,* now superseded by Ray Lewis White's quite different and superior critical edition (see Note 34).

7. "Sherwood Anderson and the Lyric Story," *The Twenties: Poetry and Prose,* edited by Richard E. Langford and William E. Taylor (De Land, Florida: Everett Edwards Press, 1966), p. 71.

8. *"Winesburg, Ohio* after Twenty Years," *Story* 19 (Sept.–Oct. 1941): 30.

9. "Sherwood Anderson," *The Liberal Imagination* (New York: Viking, 1950); revised from *Kenyon Review* 3 (Summer 1941); reprinted, Anchor Books, 1958, 28–29.

10. *Freudianism and the Literary Mind* (Baton Rouge: Louisiana State University Press, 1957; paperback, 1967), p. 248.

11. "The Sweetness of Twisted Apples: Unity of Vision in *Winesburg, Ohio,"* *PMLA* 87, No. 5 (Oct. 1972): 1101.

12. Letter to Charles and Katherine Bockler, Feb. 12, 1933, Kansas City, Mo., Newberry Library.

13. *Sherwood Anderson's Short Stories,* edited by Maxwell Geismar (New York: Hill and Wang, 1962), p. 194. All subsequent story citations, except where they are footnoted or in *Winesburg, Ohio,* are from this collection. This edition of twenty-nine stories, the only substantial collection in print, is limited not only in having but a fraction of the some eighty stories (excluding *Winesburg* tales) but also in presenting the stories without authoritative standards of editing. For example, it can be demonstrated that the editing of *The Sherwood Anderson Reader,* from which ten of the stories are selected, is unreliable.

14. *Winesburg, Ohio,* edited by Malcolm Cowley (New York: Viking, 1960), p. 57. All subsequent citations are from this edition.

15. *Letters,* p. 193.

16. "Brother Earl" (not the short story with the same title), Newberry Library.

17. *Broom* I (Dec. 1921): 148–53, included in *The Portable Sherwood Anderson,* revised edition, edited by Horace Gregory (New York: Viking, 1972), p. 336.

18. Statement included with the "Death in the Woods" MS, Newberry Library.

19. *Sherwood Anderson* (New York: Twayne, 1964), p. 88.

20. While the impressions of youths are also important in "The Egg" and "Death in the Woods," the story narrators are adults and the youths have relatively subordinate roles in the actions.

21. Howe, *Sherwood Anderson* (New York: William Sloan, 1951), p. 154.

22. The novel-length *Ohio Pagans* ms. is in the Newberry Library.

23. *Letters,* p. 387.

24. Ibid., p. 135.

25. *Horses and Men* (New York: B. W. Huebsch, 1923), p. 163.

26. *The Modern Writer* (New York: Telber, Lilienthal, 1925), p. 12.

27. Fussell, *"Winesburg, Ohio:* Art and Isolation," *Modern Fiction Studies* 6, No. 2 (Summer 1960): p. 108.

28. Ibid., p. 110.

29. *"Winesburg, Ohio* and the Rhetoric of Silence," *American Literature* 40 (Mar. 1968): 38–57.

30. Letter to Luella Williams Grace, June 30, 1930, Troutdale, Va., Newberry Library.

31. Letter to John Anderson, Nov. 1935, Ripshin, Newberry Library.

32. Fussell, *"Winesburg Ohio:* Art and Isolation," p. 111.

33. *Exit to Elsinore* (Muncie, Indiana: Ball State University Press, 1967), p. 3.

34. *Sherwood Anderson's Memoirs: A Critical Edition,* edited by Ray Lewis White (Chapel Hill: University of North Carolina Press, 1969), p. 403.

35. *Letters,* pp. 337–38.

36. "A Mountain Dance," *Vanity Fair* 29 (Dec. 1927): 59.

37. *Letters,* p. 245.

The Warmth of Desire:
Sex in Anderson's Novels

RAY LEWIS WHITE

For almost fifteen years I have enjoyed reading, editing, and teaching Sherwood Anderson's autobiographies, his short stories, his essays, and even his poetry. But a peculiar reluctance has overcome me when I have needed to reread any of the seven novels that Anderson published from 1916 through 1936. I enjoy reading these novels to find elements of autobiography or philosophy or personal charm; yet when I try to read the Anderson novels simply to have the pleasure of reading fiction, I become embarrassed for Anderson and then upset at my own embarrassment. I have worried to discover the reasons for this initial hesitation and subsequent embarrassment, and I think that I have diagnosed the problem: not so much Anderson's failures in structure nor his flaws in perspective but his treatment of sex in the novels somehow bothers me. Wondering just why troubles me; so I have reread these works specifically to study the subject of sex in Anderson's novels. My conclusions satisfy me for now, and they may stimulate other students of Anderson to their own reactions to the novels.

I

Windy McPherson's Son and *Marching Men*[1] are essentially expressions of Sherwood Anderson's years as a businessman in Ohio. Anderson probably completed these works in Elyria before his famous breakdown of November 1912, and brought the two manuscripts or typescripts to Chicago in 1913, shared the novels with friends in Chicago's Renaissance, and revised the works for publication. The two novels are most wisely viewed, I believe, as the creations of an unhappy businessman teaching himself the craft of writing long fiction in order to escape from the painful realities of buying, selling, and playing the middle-class husband and father. Anderson's attitude toward sex in these two early novels may thus reflect the confusions in his own life.

In *Windy McPherson's Son,* Sam McPherson of Caxton, Iowa, develops from a thirteen-year-old entrepreneur of newspapers into the mogul of the American firearms industry. Along the way from poor boy to captain of industry, Sam loses the sense of fulfillment and quests for ultimate meaning: "The best men spend their lives seeking truth" (p. 240). But this truth is certainly not to be found through pursuit of the sexual in life, for Sam McPherson is a moralist scarcely advanced beyond the rabid American Puritan.

Having abandoned school attendance, young McPherson "had a season of admiring his own body with its straight legs, and the head that was poised so jauntily on the body" (p. 37). The boy idealizes the stirrings of puberty, being awake at night in summer "so filled with strange longing that he would creep out of bed and, pushing open the window, sit upon the floor, his bare legs sticking out beyond his white nightgown, and, thus sitting, yearn eagerly toward some fine impulse, some call, some sense of bigness and of leadership that was absent from the necessities of the life he led" (pp. 37–38). Sam looks at village girls and "had unbelievably mean thoughts" (p. 40); he hears or knows stories of disease and unwed pregnancy; and he walks once with the banker's daughter, "one of the strange beings that had begun to bring him uneasy nights, and overcome with the wonder of it the blood climbed through his body and made his head reel so that he walked in silence unable to understand his own emotions" (p. 64). The girl kisses him and "Manhood had come to him" (p. 65)!

Warned to forego further involvement with women, Sam McPherson, still an adolescent, devotes himself to making money in farm produce and then to dealing in commodities in Chicago. The great city gives Sam money but brings out his continuing prudery, as when he wanders into a street of whorehouses: "Here and there, before and behind him, were the faces; voices called, smiles invited, hands beckoned. Up and down the street went men looking at the sidewalk, their coats turned up about their necks, their hats pulled down over their eyes. They looked at the faces of the women pressed against the little squares of glass and then, turning, suddenly, sprang in at the doors of the houses as if pursued. Among the walkers on the sidewalk were old men, men in shabby coats whose feet scuffled as they hurried along, and young boys with the pink of virtue in their cheeks. In the air was lust, heavy and hideous" (p. 127).

Anderson's hero, running from sex, plots successful schemes to become rich; thinking of money makes him feel "strangely alive and awake like a young man in love" (p. 138). Replacing sex with dollars, Sam McPherson marries into control of an arms company, thinking of the rich manufacturer's daughter more as a reputable source of babies than as a partner in sex: "He remembered how he, as a boy in the city, had run through the crowded streets fleeing from the terror of lust. He began to understand how distorted, how strangely perverted, his whole attitude toward women and sex had been. 'Sex is a solution, not a menace—it is wonderful,' he told himself . . ." (p. 191).

Fatherhood and motherhood proving impossible (Sue McPherson miscarries three babies and calls herself "unfit"),

26

Sam totally rejects women of the street or of acquaintance, fleeing the "Animal desire [that] seized and shook him, a feeling without sweetness, brutal, making his eyes burn" (p. 224). Now worth five million dollars but abandoned by his wife, Sam McPherson (like Sherwood Anderson himself) "walked out of the office, again a free man and again seeking the answer to his problem" (p. 255).

Anderson hurriedly rushes his incognito multimillionaire through a quest for meaning, apparently not to be found in laboring manually, bartending, organizing labor, reforming society, or fellowshipping with the common people—certainly not with common women. Sam wants "American men and women . . . to be clean and noble and natural, like their forests and their wide, clean plains" (p. 311). He castigates authors who treat "vice and profligacy as something, at bottom, charming" (p. 312), and he "wondered why youth could not be made to understand that sin is foul and immorality reeks of vulgarity" (p. 315). Yet he reverses direction to become totally coarse, morose, combative, and lustful. At a party, he shouts for "a woman who is a mother" (p. 330), exchanges several thousand dollars for some woman's three small children, brings them to his wife's estate in New York, and enters with her and the three children into her house and the life of meaning now found.

Because all aspects of *Marching Men* seem very primitive, very simplistic, I have wondered whether Sherwood Anderson did not write the book before he wrote *Windy McPherson's Son.* Yes or no, the writer's treatment of sex in *Marching Men* shows no improvement over that in the first-published novel.

Beaut McGregor, the hero of *Marching Men,* in several ways resembles Sam McPherson. Both characters spend their early years in small towns, they find life disorganized and meaningless, they rebel to quest for meaning—and they are unable to cope with sex. However, in creating Beaut McGregor, Anderson delineates the small town of Coal Creek, Pennsylvania, as totally unenlightened, the miners

27

and their families as animalistic, and Beaut McGregor as both insensitive and dumb.

Beaut is brutishly attractive to women, especially to pale, weak women. He may look a woman straight in the eye, but he apparently needs only to work with his widowed mother and to sit with pale, weak girls: "He got a feeling of complete, good fellowship and friendliness [from sitting] with this woman. Without knowing how the thing had been done he felt a certain pride in it" (pp. 30–31). Tempted by this pale, weak woman of Coal Creek to imagine marriage and children, Beaut prefers to dream of organizing miners into lines of mechanically marching demonstrators who, through simple marching, will reform corrupted industrialism. Given warning to avoid sex, "He thought there was sense to it. He also was afraid of the tall pale girl. Sometimes when he looked at her a pain shot through him and a combination of fear and desire gripped him. He walked away from it and went free as he went free from the life in the darkness down in the mine" (p. 56).

Arriving in Chicago in 1893, Beaut McGregor finds economic depression, so bad that "eager women driven by want sold their bodies to passersby for twenty-five cents" (p. 62). McGregor bullies his way into a warehouse job, despises disorderly humanity, and teaches himself law in order to reform society. Again tempted by women, advised to try prostitutes for uncomplicated sex, McGregor likes a friend's philosophy: "We used to have religion. But that's pretty well gone now—the old kind. Now men think about children, I mean a certain kind of men—the ones that have work they want to get on with. Children and work are the only things that kind care about" (p. 95). Giving in to his base instincts and the friend's philosophy, McGregor tries to approach a prostitute: "A fever burned in his blood. An impulse, for the moment stronger than the impulse that kept him at work over books night after night there in the big disorderly city and as yet stronger than any new impulse toward a vigorous compelling march through life, had hold of him. He hurried along filled with a lust that stultified his brain and will" (pp. 101–102). Anderson saves his hero, miraculously, by having him rob pimp-and-prostitute instead of being robbed. Now he can afford more law books!

McGregor, still "as virginal and pure as a chunk of the hard black coal out of the hills of his own state and like the coal ready to burn himself out into power" (p. 122), meets Edith Carson, a pale and weak milliner desperate to have children just when Beaut is desperate to organize all the world into marching men. Educated with Edith's savings, practicing law with enough sudden skill to expose organized crime, McGregor must now meet a woman to compete with the pale, weak milliner. And Margaret Ormsby, altruistic daughter of a millionaire plow manufacturer, is not pale, not weak, and not dull: "Her tall straight well-trained body, her coal-black hair, her soft brown eyes, the air she had of being prepared for life's challenge caught and held the attention of men" (p. 203).

Now that McGregor feels torn among wanting beautiful children from the rich and healthy Margaret Ormsby, possibly no children from the pale and weak Edith Carson, or saving the world with marching men, Anderson actually lets the two women argue before the man over their respective child-bearing potentials. The pale, weak milliner asserts her total desire for and devotion to having healthy babies; she immediately wins her Beaut McGregor; and she henceforth disappears, along with further mention of sex, from *Marching Men.* I presume that McGregor found marriage and fatherhood more permanent answers to the natural disorganization of life than his doomed, unnatural conception of the marching men.

Thus, viewed from the perspective of Anderson's handling of sex in *Windy McPherson's Son* and *Marching Men,* these two early novels show relentless moralizing on the part of an unskilled writer. Anderson does write much of the sex drive and its manifestations in these works; but his fascination appears unfortunately close to voyeurism, and his recommended sublimation of lust to child-rearing radiates the stench of sanctimony.

II

Perhaps Sherwood Anderson learned a great deal about the writing of novels from his friends in the Chicago Renaissance, or perhaps he learned a great deal about life after abandoning his business and family in 1913. Whatever the lessons, the publication of Anderson's third novel, *Poor White*,[2] starts a time of experimentation in technique and appreciation of human complexity that the author demonstrated in his long fiction in the 1920s. Especially in dealing with sex does Anderson show more sophistication than in *Windy McPherson's Son* and *Marching Men*—his "juvenilia."

Hugh McVey, the main character of *Poor White*, spends his boyhood in Mudcat Landing, Missouri, living a strange version of Huckleberry Finn's life: cursed with a drunken father and grimy poverty, Hugh is taken in and "civilized" by a Puritan woman who tries to destroy his tendency to dream. Naturally, he cannot, at nineteen, cope with sex: "A hundred new and definite desires and hungers awoke in him. He began to want to talk with people, to know men and most of all to know women, but the disgust for his fellows in the town, engendered in him by Sarah Shepard's words and most of all by the things in his nature that were like their natures, made him draw back" (p. 20).

McVey becomes a wandering worker, still flees closeness to other people, and settles near Bidwell, Ohio. Unable to do more than long for the courage to meet women, he sublimates his sex drive to inventing machines, eventually gaining great wealth from his designs. Yet "Into his long and habitually cold body the warmth of desire began to creep" (p. 76); and "He thought of how powerfully he could hold the body of a woman against his own body and the spark of the fires of spring that had touched him became a flame" (p. 77).

Poor White marks a change in Anderson's handling of sex, for at last he creates a heroine as central to his story as his hero. Clara Butterworth, daughter of a rich farmer, at eighteen feels the stirring of maturity: "A greater hunger for understanding, love, and friendliness took possession of her" (p. 147). Having watched birds mate, having been kissed by a farmhand: "Without a word he took her tightly into his arms and kissed her, first upon the neck and then upon the mouth. . . . Her brown neck and one of her hard, round breasts were exposed" (p. 151); Clara feels both lust and the potential of sexual domination of males: "she tempted the young man into kissing her, and later she lay in his arms for two hours, entirely sure of herself, striving to find out, without risk to herself, the things she wanted to know about life" (p. 158).

With the invention of Clara Butterworth, Anderson creates a believable woman. Clara feels sexual need, indecision, and even lust. Not only this, but Anderson has come to appreciate the possible complexities of human sexuality. Clara is tempted at college to become the liberated woman, the unwed lover of a male friend, and the lover of the friend's lesbian sister. Humanly confused about fulfilling her needs, Clara reaches the unfortunate but expected conclusion: "I want to be married as soon as I can find the right man. It's the only thing I can do. What else is there a woman can do?" (p. 190).

Anderson now brings together Hugh McVey, still longing for but fearful of women, and Clara Butterworth, more than ever eager for marriage. There is no delay on Anderson's part: "Hugh and Clara were married in less than a week after their first walk together" (p. 271). Hugh has dramatically defended Clara's reputation, and Clara thinks that Hugh will be the best chance she will have for marriage. As Clara gradually grows to love her husband Hugh, he remains still ashamed of his lusts—and the marriage remains unconsummated, Hugh leaping from the roof of his wife's house to

31

escape her marriage bed on his wedding night. Eventually, Clara tempts Hugh to consummate the marriage in her bed. Years later, the marriage having produced one child and one current pregnancy, Hugh and Clara end romantically: "When she told him of the struggle of the man of another generation, striving to be born he put his arm about her and held her close against his long body . . . with his arm about Clara's shoulders, he went up the steps and in at the farmhouse door" (p. 371).

Marred by this golden-sunset ending, *Poor White* demonstrates Anderson's progress in picturing human beings confronting and dealing with their sexual drives. The heroine, unlike the pale, weak women of *Windy McPherson's Son* and *Marching Men,* is a healthy Midwestern farm girl, as ignorant of sexual fulfillment but as lustful as the Midwestern hero. Neither hero not heroine can seriously think of satisfying their lusts outside of marriage, and Anderson can as yet justify sex in marriage only through child-begetting. With his next novel—fourth of seven—Anderson would liberate himself and his characters into realistic sexual attitudes.

It is ironic that such realistic sexual liberation should occur in Sherwood Anderson's most fanciful novel, *Many Marriages.*[3] The two most frequently recurring terms in *Many Marriages* are "body" and "fancy," and the subject is merely the liberation of John Webster's body through sudden self-acceptance of his imagination. *Many Marriages* opens like a fable: "There was a man named Webster lived in a town of twenty-five thousand people in the state of Wisconsin. He had a wife named Mary and a daughter named Jane and he was himself a fairly prosperous manufacturer of washing machines" (p. 3). Webster differs from Anderson's earlier heroes in not having been both poor and pure; he inherited his factory, he attended college, and as a young man he accepted and satisfied his sexual impulses. Now financially sound, almost forty years old, husband of Mary Webster and father of seventeen-year-old Jane Webster, Anderson's fictional character imitates his creator and abandons a stifling situation for personal freedom.

The plot of Anderson's novel is uncomplicated. John Webster awakens to his sexual unfulfillment, has an affair with his secretary Natalie, informs his wife and daughter of the new direction of his life, and takes Natalie away with him to live freely and fully, his wife thereupon killing herself and his daughter awakening to admiration of her father's action and her own sexual needs. The fable-like quality of *Many Marriages* is reflected in the details of this simple plot: for example, Webster's middle-aged conversion is sudden and complete; his declaration of independence is melodramatic (he extols sexual freedom to his wife and daughter while nude in his bedroom, which is decorated with candles and a Virgin Mary statue); and his final action is to ride the eastbound train at dawn with his secretary-lover. Yet *Many Marriages* is Anderson's first wise statement of a believable sexual problem and solution.

John Webster's problem is not fear of sex or lack of sex; rather, he has displaced sex with social and financial success. His life at middle age is emotionally sterile, his wife having accepted marriage with him under social pressure and sex with him as fit only for breeding. Webster is stricken with self-understanding of his barren life in his factory office, starts to contemplate human bodies as houses of human souls, and determines to cleanse his own soul-house: "His own body, that was now naked, was a house. He went and stood before a mirror and looked at himself. His body was still slender and healthy looking, outside. . . . 'A kind of house cleaning is going on. My house has been vacant now for twenty years. Dust has settled on the walls and furniture. Now, for some reason I do not understand, the doors and windows have been thrown open. I shall have to scrub the walls and the floors, make everything sweet and clean. . . . Then I shall invite people in to visit me' " (p. 23).

The immense progress that Anderson shows in picturing

Webster's awakening is his hero's knowledge that "there are no good people, only beautiful ones" (p. 68); that the sex act cannot be degrading: ("Then he laid her down upon the grass. It was an experience with a woman new in his life. After their first love-making and when their passions were spent she seemed more beautiful to him than before" [pp. 70–71]); and that breeding children is dumb enough reason for sex: "Perhaps Natalie would have a child. It did not matter" (p. 71). Most important to *Many Marriages,* however, is the hero's breadth of sexual acceptance. Early in the novel Anderson states his theme and then reiterates it until his hero faces renewed life at dawn riding eastward: "Loving Natalie did not preclude the possibility of his loving another, perhaps many others. 'A rich man [in emotions] might have many marriages,' he thought. It was certain that the possibility of human relationship had not even been tapped yet. Something had stood in the way of a sufficiently broad acceptance of life. One had to accept oneself and the others before one could love" (p. 72).

It would be tempting to assume that the only book by Sherwood Anderson truly popular in his lifetime is a novel even more sex-oriented than *Many Marriages.* However, *Dark Laughter*[4] was simply well promoted by the publisher into good sales; the plot and theme of *Dark Laughter* are much less salacious than those of *Many Marriages.* Perhaps Anderson wanted to create a more realistic, less fanciful statement of his developing philosophy of sex. Whatever the author's reasons, in *Dark Laughter* Anderson presents basically the same ideas of physical frustration and fulfillment; but he deals here with characters and sexual motivations more sophisticated than in the earlier novels.

Bruce Dudley, the hero of *Dark Laughter,* is a possible version of John Webster after that character leaves the washing machine factory in *Many Marriages.* Formerly John Stockton, a newspaper writer in Chicago, Bruce Dudley abandons his wife Bernice in order to find more fulfillment

34

than Chicago, Bernice, and sophisticated friends can provide. Bernice, also a newspaper writer, is talented, liberated, intellectual, sexually well adjusted, but not exciting to her husband: "They had been that kind in their relations to each other—he and Bernice—had got started together that way and had kept it up" (p. 19).

Anderson has this hero, tired of equality in marriage, simply abandon his liberated wife with no regrets to start the quest, this time for a more primitive philosophy of sex. Bruce Dudley drifts down the Mississippi River to New Orleans, where he hears and admires the uncomplicated, unsophisticated "dark laughter" of the blacks there: "Across the street, in another room, a nigger woman of twenty arises at five and stretches her arms. . . . Sometimes she sleeps alone but sometimes a brown man sleeps with her. Nigger girl with slender flexible body" (p. 79). Envying this primitive acceptance of sexuality but remaining strangely continent, Bruce settles in Old Harbor, Indiana, town of his youth, to work in an automobile wheel factory and absorb another example of primitivism. Old Sponge Martin, craftsman of wheel lacquering, and his old wife copulate wildly four times weekly on piles of rotted sawdust near the river. Anderson's hero craves such direct coupling and waits patiently for his own more perfect sex partner.

The heroine of *Dark Laughter* is Aline Grey, wife of Fred Grey, owner of the factory where Bruce works. Aline has always had money, she is well educated, she has traveled in Europe, she has rejected lesbian advances, she is comfortably married, she is childless ("Hadn't Fred touched her deeply enough?" [p. 136]), and she is bored. Fred Grey is dull, interested in his factory, and apparently no challenge at all to Aline, who needs the sexual spark of Bruce Dudley to light her passion. Hiring Bruce as her gardener, Aline soon leads him into her bed: "How very gentle and strong he was! At least she had made no mistake" (p. 266); "She had been a child and now she was a woman" (p. 267); and "Now she

35

would have a child, a son perhaps. That was the next step —the next event. One cannot be so deeply stirred without something happening . . ." (p. 257).

Aline, awakened and pregnant with Bruce's child, leaves Old Harbor with him; and Fred Grey, having thought of murdering Bruce Dudley or himself, apparently accepts with regret losing his wife to the sexier man. Anderson makes no promise that this hero and heroine shall remain afire for each other. He merely demonstrates in *Dark Laughter* that love or marriage without the sexual flame is unsatisfying and that both man and woman must seek perhaps "many marriages" to keep the love aflame.

III

Seven years passed until Sherwood Anderson published another novel. During the years from 1925 to 1932, the writer became involved in small-town journalism, extensive lecturing on authorship, and the labor movement. In *Beyond Desire*[5] Anderson shuns the major issue of Socialism/Communism while gingerly exploring America's economic and social problems. The major character in *Beyond Desire* demonstrates Anderson's return to the basic noble hero of *Marching Men,* but a hero flawed and humanized by his sexuality as in *Poor White* and *Many Marriages.*

Red Oliver of Langdon, Georgia, the college-educated son of a middle-class physician, has remained inexperienced in sex, in the South and even when visiting a whorehouse as a student in the North. Returned to Georgia, Red envies a Midwestern college friend who writes erotic letters about his new sex partner: "Red gathered that the little dark school teacher Neil had found was of some new world he himself wanted to get into. . . . Neil even tried to describe the feeling in his fingers when he touched her body, the warmth of her flesh, the sweetness of it to him. Red himself hungered with all his being to find such a woman for himself but never did.

Neil's letters made him also hungry for some relationship with life that was sensual and fleshly but beyond just flesh" (p. 6). Red Oliver and other characters in this novel work through the idea that "there was something beyond desire, but that you had to satisfy desire and understand and appreciate the wonders of desire first" (p. 9).

Much as he resembles Sam McPherson and Beaut McGregor in hoping to solve humanity's problems, Red Oliver has no program, no such plan as raising healthy children or lining up marching men into a new order. He is created heroic but human, determined but puzzled, lustful but hesitant. Although attracted to women workers in cotton mills in Georgia, Red has his first sex experience with the local librarian, as desirous and inexperienced as himself, copulating with her once at night on a library table. Apparently this one adventure in sex is all that Red Oliver shall have, for he obliquely becomes a strike leader in North Carolina and is killed by the militia leader in an oppression of Communists.

Beyond Desire clearly could not be built entirely around the meager story of Red Oliver, and it is in creating his secondary characters that Sherwood Anderson's attempt to handle sex maturely most brightly shines. Using the lives of these other characters to show the manifestations of sex and the need of all people for something "beyond desire," Anderson devotes lengthy sections of his novel to minor characters. For example, some of the mill girls enjoy quasi-sexual friendships: "She'd rub Grace all over. She didn't exactly feel her. Every one said that knew that Doris had good rubbing hands. She had strong quick hands. They were alive hands. What she did to Grace she did also to Ed, her husband, when he was off on Saturday night and they slept together" (p. 77). The librarian, Ethel Long, before seducing Red Oliver on her library table, fights her way out of being raped by a businessman in Chicago; after sex with Red, she fights off her stepmother: "She was soft and pleading. Now her hand had begun to caress Ethel. It was creeping down along her body, over her breasts, over her hips. Ethel remained rigid. She felt cold and weak" (p. 221). And Molly Seabright, cow-leading mountain girl who tries to shelter Red Oliver from the police and help with the coming revolution, valiantly fights against rape by a wild mountain boy.

Yet Anderson remains slightly the moralist in his treatment of sex in *Beyond Desire*. There must, his very title asserts, be commitment to purpose or will beyond fulfillment of sexual need. He still cannot write comfortably of sex merely for pleasure and without so-called higher goal. In *Kit Brandon*,[6] his final novel, Anderson remains squeamish; but *Kit Brandon* is tough, cynical, and modern about sex—an attitude seldom found in Anderson's fiction.

Kit Brandon, sharing the narrator's car on a long trip, recounts enough of her life for the uncomplicated plot of Anderson's seventh novel. Poor Blue Ridge Mountain girl escapes into cotton mill, then into marriage with rich bootlegger's son, and then into rumrunning during Prohibition. The narrator embellishes Kit's story with details of mountain, factory, and road, giving the patina of economic corruption to a history of rags to haute couture.

After being fondled by a townsman visiting her whiskey-making father, Kit undergoes attempted incest by her father as the two wash nude in a mountain stream: "He gathered cold water in his cupped hands and began to bathe her, the cold water falling down over her slender shoulders. His fingers touched her flesh. . . . She grew suddenly alarmed and ran from him" (p. 34). As a factory worker, Kit learns more of life, that sex can be bought, that beauty can be paid for. Yet "Although she had, for herself, within herself, no special call toward men, they seemed to want her" (p. 50). Eventually Kit Brandon does have sex, choosing—interesting reversal in Anderson—a sickly, pale young tubercular man who seduces her on a grassy hillside in moonlight and immediately talks of life's meaning.

Not deeply affected by the dying boy, Kit marries for money, having examined her needs rationally: "There was her straight slender young body, white flesh, straight legs, slender ankles. She did not spend much time dreaming of strong male arms about her, the brave male protecting the shrinking female. She was getting along a little in a matter of growing importance to herself, beginning to want something that some man might—by a conceivable chance—she having aforesaid nice legs, arms, little hard breasts just budding, etc.—help her to get" (p. 103).

Unable or unwilling to have a child to continue the dynasty of Tom Halsey, bootlegger with aristocratic intentions, Anderson's heroine gives herself one quick sex act with a total stranger and then apparently gives up sexual intimacy with all people forever in order to drive powerful cars loaded with illicit whiskey. The author creates a nightmare picture of gangsterism and eternal nighttime car driving. The whiskey empire collapsed, Kit Brandon still admires the bitter, tough, practical, business basis of life. Unable to have the idealized love affairs that other people claim to want, Kit will probably survive well emotionally. Although her calling card could read "Kit Brandon, Traveling," Anderson wants his heroine to have more in life; and he ends his final novel with still one more example of free sentimentality. Having consoled a runaway rich boy and having seen some rough workman gently touch his pregnant wife's body, Kit yearns toward the finer in life: "She had been carried out of herself and her own problem and into the life of another puzzled human. There were people to be found. She would get into some sort of work that did not so separate her from others. There might be some one other puzzled and baffled young one with whom she could make a real partnership in living" (p. 373). The end is cautious hope, not likely chance.

The counterarguments to my view of sex in Sherwood Anderson's novels are many. Among them: to isolate the author's treatment of sex from all of his other purposes in fiction distorts artistic integrity. I agree. To base my view of sex in Anderson's novels primarily upon the behavior of his heroes takes attention from the sexual natures of his heroines. I agree. To wish that an author born in 1876 and publishing novels from 1916 through 1936 had been as liberated as in 1976 is wishful thinking. I agree. But Sherwood Anderson claimed and is given credit for helping bring honest use of sex into American literature. I say yes, but not through the ill-conceived and sentimentalized plots and characters of his seven novels.

Instead, Sherwood Anderson brought to American literature a new way of writing short stories—stories totally of character instead of plot. In his best short fiction, Anderson was able to create brilliantly the effects of sexual adventures and sexual frustration in human beings. In novels, the writer's various messages—taught always through magnified heroes and heroines—overwhelm the artistic wisdom of character creation. I have emphasized the sexual adventures of many of the minor characters in Anderson's novels, suggesting that these brief stories often handle sex interestingly and believably. When sex must become heroic and novel-length, Anderson does slip into moralizing, sentimentalizing, and philosophizing. There are indeed certain progressions in Anderson's writing of sex from 1916 through 1936, but it is in the short stories that I see honesty and dignity and beauty in Sherwood Anderson's writing of sex.

NOTES

1. *Windy McPherson's Son* (New York: John Lane, 1916) and *Marching Men* (New York: John Lane, 1917).
2. *Poor White* (New York: B. W. Huebsch, 1920).
3. *Many Marriages* (New York: B. W. Huebsch, 1923).
4. *Dark Laughter* (New York: Boni and Liveright, 1925).
5. *Beyond Desire* (New York: Liveright, 1932).
6. *Kit Brandon* (New York: Charles Scribner's Sons, 1936).

Talbot Whittingham and Anderson: A Passage to *Winesburg, Ohio*

WALTER B. RIDEOUT

One of the puzzling aspects of Sherwood Anderson's literary career has been the apparent suddenness with which, so near the beginning of it, he made a kind of aesthetic quantum jump from his apprentice novels, *Windy McPherson's Son* and *Marching Men,* published in 1916 and 1917 respectively, to his masterpiece, *Winesburg, Ohio,* published in 1919. It is even more puzzling when one goes behind publication dates to composition dates; for though he had written some kind of draft of both novels before he abandoned his career as an independent businessman early in 1913, he made his last revisions in each novel manuscript after he had begun writing the Winesburg stories in the autumn of 1915. The lateness of these last revisions can of course be explained by his difficulties in finding a publisher for the novels, for it was not until February 28, 1916, that the John Lane Company contracted with the author to publish *Windy McPherson's Son* and gave him a month in which to put his manuscript in final shape.[1] Nevertheless, the question remains: how could An-

41

derson "jump" from the first two novels, with their promise and yet their deficiencies, to the mature artistry of *Winesburg, Ohio?* Ultimately, the question is as unanswerable as the similar one of how William Faulkner could leap from his first three uneven novels to the extraordinary achievement of *The Sound and the Fury;* however, in Anderson's case at least part of the answer can be learned from his attempts, just before beginning the Winesburg stories, to create an artist figure resembling himself, especially, but not solely, in his unpublished fourth novel named for that figure, *Talbot Whittingham.* In that novel and figure he can be seen making a passage to *Winesburg, Ohio.*

Since few people have had the opportunity to read this unpublished novel, the text of which is now available through the efforts of Gerald Nemanic,[2] it is necessary first to describe it in some detail. *Talbot Whittingham,* which seems to have been written between, roughly, the spring of 1914 and the early summer of 1915, is the one full-length novel among the many manuscript fragments concerning a man by that name which Anderson produced over perhaps as much as two decades.[3] The man in the fragments is not always the same person, but the large amount of Whittingham material suggests that at least originally this character had some special significance for its author. That significance may readily be surmised. Whereas, when published, *Marching Men* would describe the development of a largely invented labor leader and *Windy McPherson's Son* that of an only partially invented businessman, *Talbot Whittingham* traces the growth of a writer, one who despite obvious differences in external life seems often a projection of his creator's inner existence.

Although the brief Book 1 of the *Talbot Whittingham* manuscript is missing, some of its events can be reconstructed from references in the remaining four books and from a report that Anderson's friend Marietta Finley, a professional manuscript reader, prepared in "about 1916."[4] Talbot, son of an "umbrella-thief" father and a musician mother, spends his childhood in "a stuffy little apartment in New York," where the mother tries to create a salon from "an indiscriminate lot of art hangers-on" and achieves only an "abnormal, sickly atmosphere." One night the boy listens intently as a drunken youth urges him to be an artist, explaining that it is the artist alone who, though he may not understand "the law of life," knows that there is such a law which orders the mystery of existence. (Only Jesus of Nazareth, the omniscient narrator comments, would have understood this law, though a sense of it comes at times to the artist "in flashes" because of his desire to communicate with others through artistic "form.") When Talbot is twelve, his father disappears, and his mother, having discovered "her affinity in the person of a wealthy Breakfast Food man," commits him to the care of her former patron, Billy Bustard, a shy, middle-aged baker in the small Ohio town of Mirage, a name in keeping with the sardonic tone in which Book 1 appears to have been at least partly narrated.

Book 2 describes, in a series of episodes, Talbot's life in Mirage from age twelve to eighteen as he begins to develop toward what he eventually will become, a "master artist." Talbot, the narrator explains, has a "double nature." On the one hand, he is self-centered, arrogant, and manipulative of others, especially of Billy Bustard, who supports him in a lazy life with a large monthly allowance; on the other hand, he is imaginative, inquisitive and sensitive about life, and sometimes inwardly insecure despite his outward self-assurance. Thus he embodies in surrogate form the conflict between the success-seeking and the dreamy Anderson of the author's Clyde years. Through his relationships with various inhabitants of Mirage, Talbot begins to mature. Bruce Harvey, a man totally devoted to horses and harness-racing, urges him to be hard and relentless as a driver in the race of life. With a strong, imaginative girl named Jeanette Franks he vies as a teller of wild adventure tales until she enters sexual maturity, becomes pregnant by the local barber, and is forced into marriage with him. Another girl, Lillian Gale,

43

provides Talbot with his first sexual conquest, and Kit Donahue, a tough, virginal waitress, gets drunk with him one
night while "they were trying to get at an understanding of
each other and, through each other, of all men and women"
who must live in the "modern world." Then Billy Bustard's
brutal old father, Tom, returns to Mirage, rather like Huck
Finn's Pap to St. Petersburg, demands money from his son,
and tells Talbot to get out. Frightened by the man's threats,
Talbot borrows Bruce Harvey's revolver, deliberately kills
Tom, is exonerated on the false grounds that he was defend-
ing his benefactor, and with a gift of $1,500 from the embar-
rassed Billy leaves Mirage on the advice of the town's one
Socialist, who shrewdly perceives that secretly the boy re-
gards the murder as his "passport to manhood."

Books 3 and 4 detail the sequence of experiences in Chicago that over several years leads Talbot further toward an
artist's career. On the train from Mirage to Chicago he meets
and is attracted to a frank, courageous young woman who
has left schoolteaching in an Indiana town for a try at becoming a painter; but once in the city Talbot, living on Billy's gift,
forgets her and responds to his double nature, satisfying his
aggressiveness by acting as a sparring partner at a boxing
academy and his curiosity about human beings by standing
"at street crossings and looking at people," the latter being
a "passion with Talbot all of his days" and "his way of going
to school." Soon he begins the daily practice of writing down
some of his thoughts, and in a dark street one rainy night he
has a visionary experience. Suddenly "all the men and
women he had ever known seemed to press in about him"
and "with their eyes and their hands" to plead with him to
be their voice: " 'Do not think of your own life but lend your
brain and your young courage to us. Help us that we may
make ourselves understood; that all men and women may
make themselves understood.' " Shortly thereafter, however,
he joyfully beats two men in a fight over a dancehall girl but
by chance again meets the woman from Indiana. The latter
explains to him bitterly that she has failed as an artist both

because the modern woman is still too hampered by her traditional social role and because women will perhaps always be prevented by their biological role from achieving what the male as true artist can achieve, even if his dedication destroys him—the expression through himself of "the very spirit of his times and people."

Despite these steps on the way, however, Talbot's journey toward becoming a master artist is not direct. Through an acquaintance named Billows Turner, a gifted if eccentric advertising man, he drifts with the moneymaking spirit of the times into the advertising firm of Lester & Leach. Here he is financially successful, but he soon begins seriously to question "the meaning of his life." He becomes involved at the office in a long-standing quarrel between an exponent of Christ's teachings and a disciple of Nietzsche. The former insists equally on Jesus's "idea of infinite pity" and his tough-minded saying (from Luke 9:60), "Let the dead bury the dead"; the latter dismisses Christianity as sentimentality and, briefly taking Talbot on a drinking spree before hurrying nervously home to his wife, lectures his saloon audiences on the necessity of an "army of individualists," of "natural men" dedicated to following their instincts, whether to become artists or murders. Continuing the spree on his own, Talbot late that evening wildly accosts six separate people and attempts to make each perceive that he or she is a "grotesque," having been made so by the ugliness and deadness of life. Then he stalks a drunken merchant through the streets of Chicago's North Side with the purpose of killing him, obscurely feeling that this extreme act will somehow clarify his own confusion.[5] About to assault the businessman, however, he suddenly conceives of another bizarre way by which he can objectify to his maddened satisfaction Christ's "terrible saying," "Let the dead bury the dead"; and he at once goes to Turner's house to obtain his assistance in the scheme, a mass sale of inexpensive cemetery lots that will let Talbot view crowds of the living paying money toward their deaths. When carried out, the sale is very profitable for Talbot, but paradoxically it also softens the hatred he has developed against human beings as physically ugly and spiritually dead.

Book 5, the time of which is set eleven years after Talbot's first coming to Chicago, consists solely of two contrasting meetings between him and a woman. In the first he dines at a restaurant with Adelaide Brown, a wealthy dilettante more interested in artists than their art, who, as Talbot has told her, has "never done anything bold and beautiful" in her life. Just as he has cruelly forced her to admit that she does not have the courage to enter an affair with him, he catches sight of the Indiana woman, now named for the first time as Lucile Bearing, entering the restaurant with a little foreign-looking man as escort. Talbot sends Adelaide away and turns to Lucile, who, his artist's nature recognizes, has been defeated by life and yet has had the courage to accept that defeat. Seating her at a restaurant table and ignoring her angry escort, he describes to Lucile his frequent daydream of seeing her enter a long room out of a misty night, lovely of feature and with droplets of mist in her hair and on her coat that sparkle in the flames of the fireplace. The three people leave the restaurant, and as they walk toward Lucile's apartment through a misty evening, the escort becomes increasingly enraged, suddenly draws a revolver, shoots her, and runs off. Though wounded, Lucile continues to walk with Talbot to her apartment. Talbot insists on entering the apartment first, finds it, as he had hoped, a replica of the setting in his daydream, and, when the dying Lucile enters, perceives this woman who has accepted defeat to be as beautiful in actuality as in his fantasy. Then as the fireplace dances on the droplets of mist in her hair, Lucile, appearing to have "grown suddenly younger, taller and straighter," smiles at him for a moment and falls to the floor dead.

Such a summary of the book's action suggests why Anderson seems never to have submitted the manuscript to a publisher. As he himself presumably recognized, the novel has serious flaws. Not only is the ending contrived and melo-

46

dramatic, but Lucile Bearing, who is given only three scenes in the narrative, functions largely as a mechanical device for charting the development of Talbot's understanding as an artist, her unselfish death being apparently so placed as to balance out in both the novel's structure and its ethical concerns Talbot's selfish act of murder. Almost as mechanical is the Jesus-Nietzsche debate. The values ascribed to Jesus in a series of references throughout the manuscript are affirmed at the end when Talbot links his perception of the beauty hidden in defeat with his recognition that Christ wanted men and women to live in the present, not the past; but Anderson's handling of concepts is simplistic and obvious, and the "defeat" of Nietzscheanism is an easy, even unfair one. Perhaps the major defect of the novel is the uncertain presentation of the protagonist. In the long Book 2 set in Mirage, Talbot's double nature is awkwardly reflected in an inconsistent tone. Instead of being a coherent, though complex, personality, Talbot is at times described, sardonically, as one who exploits Billy Bustard, contrives a leadership image of himself among his fellows, and murders Tom Bustard with no sense of guilt, while at other times he is described, sympathetically, as one who is sensitive toward others and puzzled about life. In the Chicago books the tone shifts again as the narrator moves waveringly from a detached, somewhat condescending attitude toward Talbot to, as he comes closer to his creator's age and condition, an open approval of him, exemplified by pronouncements like, "Such men as Whittingham know everything. They confound us with the strength and insight of their glances."

Talbot Whittingham reveals much, perhaps more than intended, about Anderson's feelings and attitudes at this point in his life. The explicit assignment of a double nature to Talbot suggests how aware he was of having been himself inwardly divided in his Clyde years and later, while the psychic melodrama of such scenes as Talbot's stalking of the merchant or his sale of the burial lots is probably a gauge of the frenzied hatred of self and others that would sweep over

Sherwood from time to time in reaction to his advertising job. The "argument" of the novel, too, reflects Anderson's own conviction that entering the artist's vocation could resolve divisions, conflicts, frustrations within the self; yet in the form in which he embodies this argument there is a curious ambivalence that seems to result as much from uncertainty of concept or attitude as from the inadequate technical skill of an apprentice novelist.

Overtly the argument of the book leads toward a particular conception of the artist. In this conception the artist is connected with others, shares a common humanity with them, indeed can create his art only out of their lives and his understanding of their lives. This is what is asserted in Talbot's visionary moment in the Chicago night when all the people he has known seem to plead to him to be their voice, in Lucile Bearing's anguished admission that a man, if not a woman, can express the very spirit of his times and people, and in Talbot's ultimate penetration into the meaning of the grotesque. It is implied also in the series of admiring references to Jesus running through the novel and in the rejection of the Nietzschean view. This admiration of Jesus as one whose sayings and life were works of art, furthermore, is not only Talbot's or the omniscient narrator's; it was Anderson's as well. George Daugherty, Anderson's friend at the Critchfield advertising agency, recalled that while Sherwood was living in the lodging house at 735 Cass Street his "passing interest in Nietzsche . . . [was] awakened" and that "he bought a New Testament, applied himself to it, and informed the copy department that he 'was sold on Jesus Christ'." Daugherty's memory of Anderson's interest in Jesus at that time is confirmed by the fellow lodger Jack, whose drunkenness first from liquor then from life would prompt the story "Drink" in *Winesburg, Ohio,* and who later reminded Sherwood that in their Cass Street days he had "personally told [Jack that] Jesus was a great poet."[6]

But there are elements in *Talbot Whittingham* that contradict this argument. Talbot's deliberate murder of Tom Bustard is closer to Nietzsche's will to power than to Jesus's infinite pity, and far from ever feeling guilt for his act Talbot instances it to Adelaide Brown in his mature years as a "bold and beautiful" thing to have done.[7] And if he treats Adelaide Brown with what the narrator calls the "strange cruelty that is a part of such natures" as Talbot's, certainly his disregard in the book's concluding scene for the dying Lucile Bearing would appear, in realistic terms, self-regarding to the point of inhumanity were not that scene so obviously a maneuver by the author to provide Talbot and the reader with a climactic revelation. Especially noteworthy in a novel ostensibly asserting the closeness of artist and other men and women is Talbot's actual isolation from others. Such family ties as he originally had are permanently broken when he comes to Mirage at twelve; he establishes few close relationships among the townspeople and even these are abruptly severed by his act of murder; he forms no more than acquaintanceships among the men he works with in Chicago; his attitudes toward most of the women he meets in the city—the dancehall girl, a woman at his rooming house, Adelaide Brown—vary from mere tolerance to contempt, and that toward Lucile Bearing is essentially exploitative, however Anderson might have wished it to be regarded. Perhaps Talbot's isolation reflects Anderson's own intense desire to be free of family and business impediments in order to devote himself to writing, but in terms of the "meaning" of the novel it is as though the author of *Talbot Whittingham* were caught between competing conceptions of the artist. On the one hand, the artist is a being beyond good and evil in his personal life, the "master artist" whose gifts set him apart from other human beings; on the other hand, the artist is one who, in Lucile Bearing's words, must "give his life" in order to "make the world understand in him what there is in all men and women and what, in their own persons, they cannot understand." Perhaps Anderson himself recognized the warring impulses in the book as yet another reason for his dissatisfaction with it. At any rate, *Talbot Whittingham* would

49

not be submitted for publication, and in practical terms Anderson was faced either with finding an approach and a form that would reveal the essence of his artistic development more successfully, or with abandoning this subject.

Actually what he was looking for was there, almost realized, not yet recognized, in the unpublished and unpublishable manuscript. The chief significance of *Talbot Whittingham* is its attempt to handle materials that would eventuate in two of his best books. Early in the 1920s he would return to the characters in the manuscript as the basis for some of the tales that would make up *Horses and Men* (1923). The bold imaginative girl Jeanette Franks foreshadows the attractive and pathetic May Edgely of " 'Unused'." The Bruce Harvey scenes, with their emphasis on the satisfaction that "horse talk" and harness racing provided townsmen in Anderson's youth, look toward "I'm a Fool," while a few details, such as Talbot's desire to be with horses in a barn on a stormy night, reappear in that highly personal tale "The Man Who Became a Woman." Particularly obvious is the resemblance of the final scene in *Talbot Whittingham* to its more successful reworking as "The Man's Story." The fact that this last tale would remain one of Anderson's favorites suggests that his unpublished novel had indeed a psychic value for him much exceeding its aesthetic achievement. That psychic value is especially manifested in the striking relationships between the Mirage section, significantly the longest by far of the five books, and *Winesburg, Ohio,* the various tales of which would begin almost to flood from his imagination only a few months after he had written *Talbot Whittingham.*

There is, to begin with, the close similarity of setting. Although the name "Mirage" is satiric rather than, like "Winesburg," evocative, it refers to the same kind of small town in the same part of Ohio. Mirage is a rural community connected to the outside world by trains but with an essentially preindustrial economy. There are a town hall, a Main Street, a hotel for travelers, a fairgrounds, a cemetery; just outside the town begin the fields, meadows, patches of woods. As Winesburg would, in fact, Mirage much resembles Clyde in its geography. Though Clyde has no Pennsylvania Street, it has, as does Mirage (and Winesburg), a Buckeye Street; the Main Streets of Clyde and Mirage slope downward from the town hall to the railroad tracks; in each case the cemetery lies beyond the tracks in the north part of town. The inhabitants of Mirage, furthermore, bear Clyde names in many instances and some exhibit Clyde characteristics. Barley Miller, son of the Mirage butcher, presumably received his first name from Barley Mann, son of the Clyde butcher, and his last from such a Clyde citizen as Harkness Miller; Salty Adair, Mirage's shoemaker, may get his name from "Body" Adare, in whose saloon young Sherwood, when he was a newsboy, used to sell off his last newspapers for the day; Bruce Harvey—the real Frank Harvey was a partner in Harvey and Yetter's livery stable—habitually howls out an Indian war cry in the excitement of a harness race as did Clyde's George Crosby. So close is the Mirage milieu to remembered folkways that, as though his reader were a fellow townsman, Anderson could refer to fictitious community landmarks without bothering to describe them, simply to "Turner's Grocery" or "the alley that turns out of Main Street by Nichols Tailor Shop." Only lightly masked by invented names, his home town stood in the eye of Sherwood's memory, a background against which to move the part-imagined, part-remembered character of Talbot Whittingham.

Occasionally the distance between townsman-author and townsman-character narrows suddenly in the manuscript. At one point the omniscient narrator drops his intermittently sardonic tone and, as though he were writing a first draft of *Sherwood Anderson's Memoirs,* asserts that Talbot's boyhood in Mirage "was for him the great romantic epic of his life, the period about which he was never afterward sure, a time when fancy took on a reality that was truth and that left a mark on the growing man and artist that was never after-

51

ward effaced." Thereupon the narrator interrupts his narrative with an essay in praise of the American village, beginning with the statement that Talbot "was, in later life, like most of us who live in cities, a man who looked lovingly back upon his days in an American small town." With Whitmanesque expansiveness Talbot's individual experience becomes generalized, since men from Michigan, Pennsylvania, Vermont, and Ohio and "western fellows who have looked out over the prairies" share in common the townsman past: " 'Tis a thing in the blood of Americans, this memory of village life." Then suddenly the abstract essay turns into a single lyric scene which in its selection and composition of detail, its diction, even its sentence rhythms is fully in the yet-to-be-achieved *Winesburg* manner.

> The young and vigorous looking man we see walking before us in the street and who is going in at the door of the great store there, half running forward, working his way through the crowd, was such a fellow and walked with such a girl but five short years ago. On an evening he went with the girl along a street over a hill and a bridge into a country road. With the girl he climbed over a fence into a field. There was a pile of brush and he set it afire. The dew wet his shoes and made a dark band at the bottom of the girl's skirt. The fire did not burn well and the young man tramped it out. With the girl he went to lean against a fence. When a team passed on the road they crouched, hiding. There was no reason for concealment but they did not want to be disturbed. They were silent, their minds alive and filled with vague thoughts. The young man thought he would cut a noble figure in the world. His thoughts were vague, now they are quite definite. Next year he thinks perhaps he may own an automobile and have a beautiful woman to live in his house. His thoughts have lost color. They are now the thoughts of a thousand young men we shall see going in at the store doors.

52

The stylistic manner is maintained only momentarily; yet in other ways as well the long Mirage section of *Talbot Whittingham* shows that, unbeknown to himself, Anderson was going toward *Winesburg, Ohio*. The novel as a whole traces into early middle age the development of a writer, and that second book shows how a town and its people influence the writer's adolescent years. Foreshadowings of particular *Winesburg* tales occur in other books of *Talbot* besides the second: out of her defeat is born in Lucile Bearing what a drunken young man, apparently borrowed from the missing Book 1, prophesies in "Tandy" for Tom Hard's little daughter, "the quality of being strong to be loved"; and Talbot's vision in Chicago of "all the men and women he had ever known" pleading to him to interpret their lives resembles the old writer's vision in "The Book of the Grotesque," the prefatory tale of *Winesburg, Ohio*. But in the Mirage section, episodic as it is in structure like a series of stories, appear several meetings with individual human beings that help shape Talbot, as similar meetings in Winesburg will shape George Willard. Though Bruce Harvey is not an isolate like *Winesburg's* Wing Biddlebaum and though his message differs from Wing's, each is fond of the young protagonist of his respective book and seeks to guide him; and Talbot's relationship with Kit Donahue will share with that of George Willard and Helen White in "Sophistication" a common interest in how men and women may understand each other in the "modern world." Most strikingly of all, the chapter describing Talbot's sexual initiation with Lillian Gale prefigures that of George with Louise Trunnion in "Nobody Knows."

A final aspect of *Talbot Whittingham* points directly toward *Winesburg, Ohio*—Anderson's concern with what he was already calling the "grotesque." Although he twice uses the term in the Mirage section, only midway into Book 4 does he begin to attach a special meaning to it. Appropriately, that special meaning appears during his night drinking spree when he runs through the Chicago streets distraught with the conviction that he is "trying to live in a dead world filled with dead men and women." Life, Talbot believes, has "twisted and maimed" the minds and personalities of the six people he accosts, making them "grotesques," mere reflections of the world's own deadness and ugliness. The only one of the six to be described at length is a woman who works in a restaurant where, persecuted by male customers, she has become obsessed with a single desire, literally to "beat down men" with an iron bar in order to begin life anew, "to stand for something," to "make her protests felt and understood." This Chicago woman would have been at home in Winesburg. Talbot's confrontation with her and the other five "grotesques" saves him that night, the author asserts, "perhaps from insanity"; for in his agitation he senses that by roughly touching the six persons, each of whom he tells is "alive but . . . not beautifully alive," he will be able to find and restore "Something sweet and precious [that] has gone out of the world." The full meaning of grotesqueness only comes to Talbot much later, however, when by perceiving the courageous beauty Lucile Bearing exhibits beneath her outward defeat, he understands that "Everything is grotesque and the beautiful is beyond the grotesque." It is the duty of the artist to break through the grotesque, which Talbot now likens to a wall surrounding each person and thing, and to discover the beauty behind it. Grotesqueness, in sum, is a universal but outward condition of the world which both defeats men's dreams and separates them as individuals; beauty is a universal but inward condition which exists beyond defeat, binds individuals into a community, and when liberated by the artist's insight, emerges out of defeat in the form of art.

In *Talbot Whittingham,* then, Anderson had told the story of an artist much resembling his inward self, had reawakened and set down memories of his home town, and had worked out a theory of the grotesque, all apparently by the late spring of 1915. But even after completing his novel he continued to "play in his fancy" with the novel's main figure, attempting to use him now as an even more direct means of self-examination. He started but seems not to have progressed far with a novel entitled *The Golden Circle,* the very first page of which confirms the intensely personal significance of the Whittingham persona for his creator.[8] Talbot is first seen standing "at the window of a room on the second floor of a frame house in the town of Winesburg, Ohio." So the evocative name has already replaced the earlier sardonic one; and the close relationship of the fictional Winesburg with the real Clyde, of Talbot Whittingham with Sherwood Anderson is drawn tighter when the description of the frame house and its setting is seen exactly to tally with 129 Spring Avenue, where the Andersons lived from 1889 onward. There is even a big beech tree in the front yard with a spring at its foot. A neighbor child had drowned in the spring, and a white-faced Mrs. Whittingham had pulled the body out.[9] Anderson was openly relying on his own psychic past, for in a clear-sighted but sympathetic way he portrays seventeen-year-old Talbot as one who continues to envy another Winesburg boy his skill at baseball while turning for compensation to the reading of books and to flamboyant daydreams so intense that they take on the vividness of actuality.

For some unknown reason *The Golden Circle* was left unfinished. Another attempt to search the author's self by means of the Talbot persona was the likewise unfinished, perhaps hardly begun, *Talbot the Actor.* Here Whittingham is introduced as a young man on the last evening of his yearlong stay in Springfield, Ohio, during which he had lived at a boarding house run by an older woman, had attended the local college, had given a speech at Commencement exercises on the Jews in modern society, and had so held the audience's attention that an enthusiastic business executive had offered him an advertising solicitor's job on the spot.[10] So many other events prior to Anderson's own Springfield year are so direct from memory that one pays particular attention to what Talbot's former army friend Bert had told him before they parted one evening "on the docks in the city of Cienfu[e]g[o]s, in Cuba," that Talbot "was always an actor." This last evening in Springfield, while he waits until time to meet a passionate town girl with whom he is having an affair, Talbot as usual is absorbed in thinking of himself, of the contradictory impulses making up his "subconscious life," impulses that he visualizes as separate people conflicting within him in a kind of psychodrama. One person is "a white bearded old man," always sternly and honestly judging others and Talbot himself, but a "laughing lustful thing" within Talbot struggles with this puritanical judge and always comes out victorious. This laughing, lustful "poet" person Talbot revealingly visualizes as a figure who physically resembles the young Sherwood Anderson, a handsome, slender youth with "black hair and burning eyes," a youth always "running, through the world, among people, through streets of towns, over hills," though to what goal Talbot does not know. Sometimes, however, this "white and pure" youth, dancing like a white streak through the world, turns abruptly into "a grotesque ugly thing." Such a metamorphosis had happened in the terrible period just before Talbot had gone into the army, when for two years he had been "a young laborer in factories" and had devoted himself to hating people. Talbot likes to think, and knows that he likes to think, of the poet rather than the grotesque ugly youth as his true self, though "One could be quite satisfied if the poet was within him occasionally." Yet other persons exist within the "highly organized" Talbot, who, the narrator comments, is becoming a type in the modern world: one is "the figure of a small white faced woman hurrying with quick frightened footsteps through of [sic] life as though wanting to escape from it quickly and another of a general, very pompous and empty headed [;] he continually strutted before people."

This self-analysis by the fictional Talbot Whittingham is striking, since seen in the closely autobiographical context of the novel fragment it confirms Anderson's capacity for both imaginative self-dramatization and for a ruthlessly honest introspection. It also confirms his interest just prior to beginning the Winesburg stories, in dealing with the inner life of a character and in discovering fictional devices for expressing that inner life. In addition the person's self-analysis suggests how closely Anderson's observation of his own psychic mechanisms was related to the creative act itself. So Talbot's emphasis on the youthfulness of his poet-self points back to the "boyishness" that repeatedly characterizes the mature artist in *Talbot Whittingham* and forward to the "young thing" within him that saves the old writer in "The Book of the Grotesque," the introductory tale of *Winesburg,* all of these instances expressing Anderson's sense of being, in terms of his own writing career, still a youth. In such ways both *The Golden Circle* and *Talbot the Actor* fragments show him, to use one of his favorite words, groping toward his master work.

Anderson's several versions of how he wrote the first story of *Winesburg* conflict with each other in details and even with obvious facts, including his specific reference in most versions to the first story as being "Hands," actually the second written after "The Book of Grotesque"; but most of the accounts agree in suggesting that at the moment he was feeling especially harassed by his advertising job. He may also have been feeling frustrated by his failure as yet to place one of his longer works with a publisher, and he could well have been dispirited that, though he had been writing steadily through the summer and into the early fall, so much of this writing did not appear to be getting anywhere. Putting aside the inconclusive experiments with Talbot Whittingham, he had started a story about a George Bollinger and an Alice Hassinger who, though each is married to another, fall desperately in love; but he could not get them beyond the point where they admit what is happening between them. Adding the pages of this failed effort to the growing pile of discarded sheets on his big worktable in the room at the top of his Cass Street rooming house, he next drove his pencil across some thirty-three sheets of yellow paper in an effort to tell about a Trigant Williams, who as a boy in an Ohio

River town lacked the courage to approach a promiscuous little girl from a rural slum, but who, with the town "fixed" in his memory even in adulthood, later became "a pagan." Then Anderson abruptly dropped Trigant Williams and tried another approach to the theme of the artist through describing the boyhood of a Paul Warden, who in one scene rejects formal Christianity because it lacks the sense of the erotic and mystical which, Paul feels, Christ himself must have had, and who in high school shows sufficient skill at drawing that a teacher encourages him to "protect your imagination." Yet the Paul Warden story did not seem to head in the right direction either, and Anderson broke it off on a final page containing a single sentence: "Paul was in a house in the city of Chicago."

That sentence may have been the last push to his imagination that he needed; for one evening in the fall of 1915 he came back wearily from the advertising office to his room in Cass Street and was seized with yet another story idea which by conscious design would allow him to unite the image of an old writer in a house in Chicago with that of a young man developing his artistic imagination in a small Ohio town named Winesburg. Turning over on his worktable the big pile of discarded sheets, Anderson took the top one—on its reverse was that sentence, "Paul was in a house in the city of Chicago"—and began to write about an old writer in a room like his own whose mind, like that of the first Talbot Whittingham, was filled with a procession of people, all the people he had ever known, all of them grotesques, who had helped a young artist to maturity and kept an old one young. He began to write *Winesburg, Ohio.*

NOTES

1. Information from a reproduction of a copy of the Memorandum of Agreement between the John Lane Company and Sherwood Anderson, generously furnished by John Ryder of The Bodley Head, founded by John Lane.

2. See Gerald Carl Nemanic, *"Talbot Whittingham:* An Annotated

Edition of the Text Together with a Descriptive and Critical Essay"
Doctoral dissertation, University of Arizona, 1969); available from University Microfilms. Quotations in my article are from this edition with the permission of Eleanor Copenhaver Anderson and Gerald Nemanic. Although Nemanic and I of necessity differ in our approaches to the novel, I am glad to acknowledge my indebtedness to his introductory essay for several suggestions.

3. The evidence concerning dates of composition of Anderson's first four novels is fragmentary, vague, contradictory, and too complicated to be rehearsed here. Mr. Nemanic tentatively dates the writing of *Talbot Whittingham* as extending from "possibly" late 1912 to "probably" 1915 or 1916. Partly on the grounds that Anderson probably completed his third novel, the also unpublished *Mary Cochran,* in the winter of 1914, I tentatively date *Talbot Whittingham* as being written within the shorter period of time. It is certain, however, that Anderson had written all or substantially all of this fourth novel before he began the Winesburg tales.

4. Nemanic, *"Talbot Whittingham,"* p. 12, fn. 21. Mr. Nemanic quotes a letter to him from William A. Sutton, who reported what Miss Finley (Mrs. E. Vernon Hahn) told him. The text of this report is given in Sutton, *The Road to Winesburg: A Mosaic of the Imaginative Life of Sherwood Anderson* (Metuchen, N.J.: The Scarecrow Press, 1972), pp. 584–88. Quotations in this paragraph are from the report except for those in the parenthesis, which are from the edited text.

5. A suggestion of how closely Anderson seems to be projecting through Talbot's action his own periods of emotional stress is the curious fact that in a novel little given to naturalistic detail the route of the hunted and hunter is traced by street names so exactly that an actual murder would have been committed in full view from Anderson's room in the lodging house at 735 Cass Street on Chicago's Near North Side. He had taken up residence there in the fall of 1914 and there began writing the Winesburg stories a year later.

6. George H. Daugherty, "Anderson, Advertising Man," *Newberry Library Bulletin,* Second Series, No. 2 (Dec. 1948): 37; letter from Bronson Gobe to Sherwood Anderson, July 15, 1921. Of Anderson's "passing interest in Nietzsche," Daughterty further states: "The only thing in the Overman's philosophy that we ever heard him quote was the assertion to the effect: This is true—but the opposite is also true, which fitted in admirably with Anderson's well-known theory of the relation of truth and romance."

7. Talbot's killing of Tom Bustard may be an echo of H. G. Wells's *Tono-Bungay* (1910), which it is likely Anderson had read in the summer of 1913. Although the circumstances differ widely and George Ponderevo, the narrator of *Tono-Bungay,* feels guilt when he commits the murder, by the time he has come to write his "autobiographical" novel, he can refer to the act with a detachment surprisingly like Talbot's: "It is remarkable how little it troubles my conscience and how much it stirs my imagination, that particular memory of the life I took." (*Tono-Bungay,* [NY: Scribner's, 1925], Atlantic Edition, vol. 12, p. 298.)

8. In "How Sherwood Anderson Wrote *Winesburg, Ohio*" (*American Literature,* 23 [Mar. 1951]: 7–30), William L. Phillips astutely argued that *The Golden Circle,* and the other uncompleted fictions here discussed, preceded *Winesburg* and formed the pile of discarded sheets on the blank back sides of which Anderson wrote many of the *Winesburg* tales. Though the argument is generally persuasive, these original pieces of writing must be dated cautiously. At least one story, narrated in the first person by an advertising man named Sidney Melville, was certainly written well after the first *Winesburg* tales were composed, since on page 7 Melville says of a party that "now that prohibition has come, everyone got a little drunk." The Eighteenth Amendment did not come into effect, of course, until Jan. 19, 1919.

9. See Sutton, *Road to Winesburg,* pp. 505–507, for accounts of the actual incident involving Anderson's mother and the neighboring Wyatt child.

10. Except for the fact that Anderson had attended Wittenberg Academy, not Wittenberg College, these events are almost unchanged autobiography from his Springfield year, 1899–1900.

Anderson and
the Problem of Belonging

WELFORD DUNAWAY TAYLOR

An inevitable accessory of centennial celebrations is the tendency to reassess. Whether the subject be personal or geographical, it seems to come with the territory. Because Sherwood Anderson's birth fell during the centennial of American independence in 1976, those who share the joint distinction of being Americans as well as Anderson devotees will doubtlessly be involved in celebrating both country and author, a process that leads, ultimately, to a consideration of the one vis- à- vis the other.

For many—particularly the young Turks who have produced myriad publications in the last decade and a half—the reassessment began a long time ago. And it would not be unfair to say that in the current centennial year of Anderson's birth these efforts are on the way to achieving the desired purpose of recognizing the extent of Anderson's artistic accomplishment and assigning his reputation to an unassailable position in American literary annals. There is no one more hopeful than I that such a feat, or even a reasonable approximation, will be achieved. But if the history of Anderson criticism has taught us nothing else, it is that all who

61

champion the cause had best keep their defenses high.

If one were to plot the history of Anderson's critical standing on a graph, the pattern would show considerable unevenness. From the critical success of *Winesburg, Ohio* in 1919 to the popular reception of *Dark Laughter* in 1925, the line would run rather consistently high as it covered the years of *The Triumph of the Egg* (1921), *Horses and Men* (1923), *Many Marriages* (1923), and *A Story Teller's Story* (1924). We would then see a downturn, as Anderson experimented with journalism in an obscure corner of Virginia (1927–31) and gradually drifted into various nonfictional modes and social causes that occupied most of his final fifteen years. In so saying, one does not forget the brilliant flashes of short-story writing found in *Death in the Woods and Other Stories* (1933) or that, given Anderson's limitations as a novelist, *Kit Brandon* (1936) can hold its own with earlier attempts within the same genre. However significant these exceptions may be, the fact remains that no significant upswing can be noted until the publication of Paul Rosenfeld's edition of the *Memoirs* in 1942. Both this event and the other milestones of primary publication in the 1940s and 1950s—Rosenfeld's *Sherwood Anderson Reader,* Horace Gregory's *Portable Sherwood Anderson,* Howard Mumford Jones's and Walter B. Rideout's edition of the *Letters*—were all well received. The same can be said of similar publications of the 1960s and 1970s.

Nevertheless, immediately following his death Anderson's ranking came under its most serious threat before or since. The chief antagonist in this sequence is without question Lionel Trilling, who signed, but never successfully delivered, the death warrant on Anderson's permanent status as a writer. It was Trilling who, after citing Anderson's failure to develop what began as "an act of will" (the paint factory episode) into "an act of intelligence," deplored the smallness and drabness of his vision and the dearth of actuality in his fiction.[1]

Such judgments seem to presage those of Irving Howe,

who, after citing "that strain of lyrical and nostalgic feeling which in Anderson's best work reminds one of another and greater poet of tenderness, Turgeniev,"[2] and even after granting a somewhat wider range of accomplishment and influence than Trilling had done, states in the final paragraph of his 1951 critical biography that Anderson's place in our culture is "only a minor one."[3]

No student of Anderson's critical reputation has failed to note the negative notes sounded by Trilling and Howe, and anyone involved in the reassessment process and in speculations for what the future may hold would do well to ponder this negative offensive. One may easily say that in light of the popularity enjoyed by Anderson in the last two decades, it matters little what was said so long ago. I would disagree for several reasons. First, Trilling and Howe were at the time they made their evaluations and remain today two of our most prestigious critics. Second, collections of Anderson criticism invariably reprint their statements, which fact reflects not only the prominence of the critics themselves, but indicates that their findings crystallize the misgivings held by Anderson's detractors in general.

There is, however, a third matter which seems to have gone without notice and which I submit lies at the heart of their critical thrust. It points up certain inherent problems posed by Anderson to the American critical establishment— problems which may spell difficulty for his permanent status in the future. Since the late nineteenth century, New York has been the center of the American literary establishment.[4] Not only have most of the large publishing houses been based there, but the tastes of the publishing industry have been largely shaped by the native New York ambience. Of all the facets of this taste, none has exerted more influence upon the New York publishing orbit than the endemic literary criticism.

I know of no better account of this cultural influence and of those responsible for its promulgation than that written by Irving Howe himself in a long essay titled "The New York

Intellectuals."[5] Professing a strong interest in politics and other branches of philosophy, this criticism is of a highly specialized sort. Hear Howe's succinct summary of its basic tenets:

> [The New York intellectuals] appear to have a common history, prolonged now for more than thirty years; a common political outlook, even if marked by ceaseless internecine quarrels; a common style of thought and perhaps composition; a common focus of intellectual interests. . . . [T]hey have a fondness for ideological speculation; they write literary criticism with a strong social emphasis; they revel in polemic; they strive self-consciously to be "brilliant". . .
>
> The New York intellectuals are perhaps the only group America has ever had that could be described as an intelligentsia . . .[6]

In the face of such a credo, we can see the figure of Sherwood Anderson—once aptly described as "[a] strange man [who] lumbered across America on Midwestern feet"[7]—as strange if not downright outlandish.

At the risk of understating, Sherwood Anderson was not the kind of writer to fare well with the New York critical establishment. In the first place, he was about the farthest one could get from the common background and upbringing which bound the New York group together. Born in the unfashionable Midwest, his education followed a sort of crazy-quilt pattern, and for a time he labored long and hard in the vineyards of philistia, where his object was not to criticize the prevailing economic order, but rather to succeed within it. After the apocalyptic moment which separated him from the world of trade—or, to be more precise, after which he subordinated that realm to the kingdom of art—he followed a course which had been charted by a variety of literary hands.

Relatively little is known of his reading, yet it is safe to assume that if he read what good Eastern intellectuals were supposed to read, he read it only because he came by it incidentally and not from any sort of group pressure. The fiction he ultimately published is decidedly unique. It is the result of one man's education and of one man's experience, and whatever influences it shows came about through sub-liminal means. The indelible imprint affixed upon this body of literature was as deserved a hallmark as that appearing upon any original creation. It grew out of the same impulse to build in one's own way that had inspired the populating of the Midwest itself. Even in Anderson's one encounter with an important Midwestern group (one of the few cultural groups ever formed in the region) one can find more examples of difference than similarity among the members. The "Robin's Egg Renaissance" of the mid-1910s in Chicago was not, and for deep cultural reasons could not, have produced a party line of the sort sketched by Howe. Neither in Ander-son nor in the writers of the Midwest as a whole could there have ever been "a common political outlook"; a self-conscious striving to be "brilliant"; or, aside from certain broad similarities of idiom and structure, "a common style of thought and composition."

Moreover, noting large national literary movements, we see Anderson conforming scarcely at all. Various attempts would make him a naturalist, a romanticist, a realist; and without fail, when such cases are made, examples are carefully selected. In other words, in a fair number of instances one will find examples of romanticism; in certain isolated and select places, realism; in still fewer, naturalism. But to fit Anderson into a category in the same manner, say, that we associate Clemens with realism, Emerson with romanticism, or Crane with naturalism would be folly.

How, then, are we to take the situation of this individualistic Midwesterner, this misfit of the Corn Belt, who so stubbornly refuses to lie in the procrustean beds in which we customarily lay those who require less alteration? From my own standpoint, Anderson must be accepted on the basis of

65

what he is and on none other. No amount of wishful thinking will turn his interests into channels in which they did not choose to go, and no amount of stretching will make him conform exactly to those norms established for defining the various literary "-isms" that ran concomitantly with his production. It also seems unfair to criticize Anderson, as Trilling does, on the bases that his work contains little of "the stuff of actuality"[8] or that he himself lacked what "We may call . . . *mind,* but *energy* and *spiritedness,* in their relation to mind, will serve just as well."[9]

Now it is well and good for Trilling and the New York critics in general to hold in high esteem those authors who faithfully render the outward features of reality, just as it is for them to admire pronounced cerebration accompanied by energy and spiritedness. What seems unacceptable in these notions is that they should be taken as the *sine qua non* of successful literature.

Let it be clearly understood that I am not charging Howe, Trilling, or any member of their school with taking a prejudicial stance in their criticism. What I am saying is that the New York critics, however enlightened and however fortified with the ideas which seem so to excite the intellectual vanguard, run as great a risk of imposing limitations upon the work they analyze as does the individual who is ignorant of such ideas, or one who argues from closely circumscribed bases such as Marxism.

But New York critics aside, we are still faced with the hard fact that placing Anderson into any neat category or consistent set of values produces an ill fit. Moreover, whether it be the New York critics or anyone else discussing him, this fact is to some degree discomforting.

The ultimate place that Anderson is to occupy in our literature will in large measure be determined by those cultural values that prevail in public taste in general and among our literary critics in particular. Those who tend to side with the New York critics and those who hold with the defenders may well have to continue the debate, despite the fact that

66

the latter seem now to be holding the field.

I suggest the possibility of an ongoing debate because the two sets of values mentioned above are by no means resolved in the national mind. Anderson is an ideal vantage point from which to view a cultural dialogue that has continued for more than three quarters of a century. The contest involves two polarities: first, what, for want of a better term, I shall call The Cult of the Knowing; second, the attitudes represented in the long raging arguments of The New Humanists.

The first group, which includes the "New York Intellectuals," as labeled by Irving Howe, can be said to have its tap root in the Enlightenment and numerous truncations in the nineteenth century where, having come to full foliage, it casts its long shadow across the preponderance of thought in the twentieth century. I speak, of course, of the notion that not only is reason man's highest and noblest faculty, but that all other faculties are to be distrusted if found in conflict with it; for reason is capable of explaining all phenomena and solving all problems.

The many forms reflecting this notion are legion to any student of the history of ideas. The "higher criticism" of the Bible, the Darwinian explanation of man's origin and nature, Freud's clinical approach to the psyche, the Comptian approach to social structure and environment, the Marxist thesis concerning the eradication of repressive social classes— all represent nineteenth century outcroppings of the general notion that nothing is to be accepted on the terms of tradition, faith, or appearance, and that not only can a self-conscious explanation be found for the human state-as-found, but a theoretical basis can be propounded which will correct the various wrongs detected.

By 1899, when Sherwood Anderson was receiving his most structured year of formal education, members of the American intellectual community were much involved with these ideas. The nature of their involvement was not merely familiarity with the theories, but in many cases involvement in actual application. There can be no doubt that Anderson was exposed to much of the new thought. His chameleon-like political convictions have been the subject of recent investigation,[10] as have the discussions of Freud among the members of the Chicago Renaissance.[11] Many of the fashionable ideas of the time were then, as now, somewhat loosely lumped together under the broad umbrella of "modernism," and room was always left for including forward-looking literary modes. Here again, we are aware of Anderson's knowledge of Emily Dickinson, Vachel Lindsay, Gertrude Stein, Carl Sandburg, Marianne Moore, and numerous other practitioners of the modernistic mode. Still, despite his exposure to the many notions of newness and even revolt that were abroad during his formative years, he seems to have responded to none in a doctrinaire way.

Strongly opposed to the doctorines of progress through science and utopia through rationalistic theory stood the New Humanists, whose guiding lights were the scholars Paul Elmer More and Irving Babbitt. In a long series of essays and books[12] More, Babbitt, and their followers expressed a distrust of rationalistic absolutes, pragmatism, and the idea that society should be remade by restrictive theories of do-gooders posing as humanitarians. They appreciated education that was well rounded, and they admired disinterestedness in making value judgments. To be valued above all else were those characteristics that were distinctly human, part of which separated man from other living things. And between man and the things of the world around him they prescribed a sympathetic balance. Far from being crusaders for any one set of ideas or beliefs—their tastes were wide ranging and eclectic—they held individual discrimination as the important arbiter. While distrusting the excesses of emotionalism, they were not intolerant of emotion as a basic human attribute.

As can be readily seen, when confronted with a set of modish ideas, especially those which attempted to reduce man and his values to so much scientific data, the New Humanists offered no inconsiderable amount of resistance.

Their arguments were well informed, urbane, and always scholarly. In retrospect, however, we can see that these qualities were partially responsible for the failure of the New Humanism to capture the public attention gained by such ideas as Darwinism, Marxism, or Freudianism.

Viewing, then, the values of The Cult of the Knowing as opposed to those of the New Humanists, where does Anderson fit? Clearly, we can agree with Trilling's statement, made in his deprecatory essay written the year after Anderson's death, that declares Anderson's connection "with the tradition of men who maintain a standing quarrel with respectable society and have a perpetual bone to pick with the rational intellect."[13] As a man at once condemned and applauded for his paucity of "ideas," we simply waste time in attempting any accommodation of Anderson with the Cult of the Knowing.

Conversely, there are those who would initially question the attempt to place him in the opposing camp of the New Humanists. And, at first glance, the distance between these cultivated minds and Anderson's hit-or-miss cultural background seems as great as that separating him from the New York Intellectuals. Yet, both he and the New Humanists viewed the early decades of the century with concern and misgiving. Both were enemies of science and materialism, and of their dehumanizing effects upon society. Both distrusted rational absolutes, and both appreciated balance and order both within man and between him and the environment. Also, both generally subscribed to those values that distinguish man from other living things and maintained that these distinctions should be nurtured and defended at all costs. Anderson and the Humanists were, in short, assuming a posture for those things, however imperfect, which were human as opposed to those that the old century had presented to the new as the ultimate in wisdom and rational thought.

But even while acknowledging such areas of overlap, it soon becomes obvious, both through inference and from ex-

69

plicit statements on the part of More,[14] that in terms of education, temperament, and approach to his craft Anderson fell far short of the ideals that the New Humanists had established. It may of course be a certain consolation to say that Theodore Dreiser, Joseph Hergesheimer, James Branch Cabell, Sinclair Lewis, and John Dos Passos, to cite but a few modern recipients of Humanistic censure, also fell short at varying degrees and for varying reasons.

Of the several articulate spokesmen in the group, More in particular addressed himself to the contemporary writers of his own country while advocating the humanistic ideal in literature. Of the writers cited, we may today find it strange that he selected Dreiser as the best of the lot. And, for whatever value old consolation prizes may retain, More acknowledged Sherwood Anderson as being Dreiser's "rival to the throne."[15] In many ways, More's assessment retains a remarkable degree of soundness after almost fifty years. He wisely noted that Anderson was "a realist . . . after a fashion, but one in whose brain the solid facts of life have an odd way of dissolving before your very eye into the clouds of dreamland."[16] He perceived, while seemingly not completely appreciating, Anderson's merging of past and present and the circularity of his fictional rhetoric. Equally perceptive is his observation that in the treatment of sex there "was something wholesome and clean in the author's attitude."[17] And, finally, he appreciated Anderson's poetic style.[18]

Where he predictably found fault with Anderson was in the latter's unlocking of the horde of his subconscious which, while likening the process to "Plato's account of the appetites that sometimes awake in a man when he falls asleep," More felt that a normal man would hold such fancies in abeyance and that in releasing them Anderson was motivated by "a kind of low vitality, a sickly feverishness of the imagination."[19] "There was the stuff of a good artist in Mr. Anderson; the pity of it is that, through indulgence encouraged by evil communications, there has come about an almost complete impotence to check the flood of animal suggestions from his subconscious self; some of his later books are a painful illustration of what 'the stream of consciousness' means when it is allowed to grow putrid."[20]

It is not surprising that the New Humanists, trailing the robes of the academy, should have found much with which to disagree in the erratic process by which a raw Midwesterner came to the realm of letters. Anderson's background did not yield that proper measure of the various humanistic disciplines nor did his temperament, either as expressed in his life style or as a literary persona, reflect the sense of poise and moderation which the humanists proclaimed as being essential to the humanistic posture.

It is, however, with the New Humanists that the problem of belonging and the problem of future assessment are drawn into the sharpest and most permanent focus. We must appreciate the areas of overlap between Anderson and the scholarly exponents of the movement such as More and Babbitt. We must see the emphasis that both placed upon the unique qualities of the individual pitted against the mechanistic ideas of absolutes as expressed in naturalism, Darwinism, and in material "progress." We must appreciate the respect that both had for the emotions as opposed to scientific data concerning the human organism and its physical world. And we must note, finally, the respect that both showed for expression in modes that reflected a tradition more poetic than factual in a scientific sense.

It is commonplace to state that Anderson felt his way into his characters in order to determine their essential "truth." His approach was anything but methodical or clinical. It was based upon inspiration and the sudden flash of intuitive insight. In short, Anderson possesses much of the humanistic quality which the more academic Humanists saw and appreciated. More's criticism of Anderson and several of his contemporaries, cited above, was delivered in 1928. By this time the movement known as the New Humanism was beginning to wear thin. Not only was a major antithetical argument building which would culminate in 1930 with *The*

Critique of Humanism,[21] but world history had taken a pronounced nonhumanistic course since the movement's beginning in the first decade of the century. For instance, the Humanists' fear of absolutes had been answered by the bloody assertion of an absolutist government in Russia. Its skepticism about the dehumanizing effects of science had been rewarded by seeing the Great War won by the most advanced of machines. And as for the proportioned life, the decade of the 1920s knew perhaps more excesses than any former time in American history. The Humanists may have scorned the Midwestern writer's disdain for Puritanism, but both were agreed that the Humanistic ideal which placed man before theory and ideal before idea was slipping away. Naturalism, picturing man and the universe in the starkest, most salacious details, was still a major force. Society was headed down a collision course toward economic collapse and moral and political confusion.

These events were watched both by Anderson and the Humanists with dismay and fear. Anderson, however, given the relatively protected atmosphere of Marion, Virginia, could stand secure within the small town ideal and express a limited degree of optimism even from the depths of the depression and from the snarls of the labor movement.

On the other hand, in the realm of criticism itself, the New Humanists saw their world collapsing. From the standpoint of political and economic crisis, the rarefied ideal of the Renaissance man enjoying the luxury of learning for learning's sake seemed remote indeed. Both More and Babbitt died in the 1930s, but not before they were forced to experience a social order that necessitated the utilitarian as opposed to the reflective. They saw the beginnings of the impersonal governmental monolith in America, and they heard the rattle of swords in Europe. And they must have looked with regret at the prominence of those schools of criticism that were redolent with the Cult of the Knowing.

Between Anderson's death and the centennial of his birth, however, this position has been mitigated to a large extent.

Historical critics (both biographers and literary historians), formalists, psychological and even textual critics have entered the picture to a greater extent than at any time during Anderson's life. With disinterested approaches, and with a minimum of ideological predilection, they have said much that has proved constructive about an author whose permanent status was still being decided.

Is this to say that their efforts in behalf of Anderson and others have made the American literary sphere a safe place for humanistic values? The answer, I believe, is a qualified no. However, in bringing back the spirit of disinterestedness, these critics have returned one of the most valuable characteristics of Humanism—one that they seem to have borrowed from Matthew Arnold. This has allowed for accepting Anderson on his own terms. It has resulted in a picture at once clearer and more complex than we would have ever known, had the detractors' word been accepted as final. In the age that lights its houses with nuclear power and sends its military personnel for walks on the moon, we despair of the time when old ideas and idea men will ever be important again, as the New Humanists insisted. But if Sherwood Anderson's current prominence is not due to the presence of the humanistic ideal among our critics, then we may at least rest assured that it may well contribute toward its re-establishment.

NOTES

1. Lionel Trilling, "Sherwood Anderson," in *The Liberal Imagination*, p. 26.
2. Howe, *Sherwood Anderson*, p. 255.
3. Ibid., p. 256.
4. Another of the New York group, Alfred Kazin, suggests that William Dean Howells' resignation from the Boston-based *Atlantic Monthly* in 1881 and his subsequent writing for New York magazines such as *Century, Scribner's,* and *Harper's* represents the beginning of the New York influence. (Howells moved to New York in 1891.) Alfred Kazin, *On Native Grounds* (New York: Reynal and Hitchcock, 1942), p. 4.
5. Irving Howe, "The New York Intellectuals," in *Decline of the New*

(New York: Harcourt, Brace & World, 1970), pp. 211–65.

6. Howe, "New York Intellectuals," pp. 211–12.

7. Evan S. Connell, Jr., review of Ray Lewis White, ed., *Sherwood Anderson's Memoirs:* A Critical Edition; *The New York Times Book Review,* Aug. 10, 1969, p. 25.

8. Trilling, p. 28.

9. Ibid., p. 26.

10. See, e.g., Rex Burbank, *Sherwood Anderson,* pp. 48–60, and G. Bert Carlson, Jr., "Sherwood Anderson's Political Mind: The Activist Years," unpublished dissertation, University of Maryland, 1966.

11. See, e.g., Frederick J. Hoffman, *Freudianism and the Literary Mind* (Baton Rouge: Louisiana State University Press, 1957), pp. 229–50, and Sutton, *The Road to Winesburg,* pp. 305–306.

12. Of these, the most helpful for defining the movement are Norman Foerster, ed., *Humanism and America* (New York: Farrar and Rinehart, 1930), and Irving Babbitt, *Literature and the American College* (Boston: Houghton Mifflin Company, 1908).

13. Trilling, p. 26.

14. See especially Paul Elmer More, "Modern Currents," in *The Demon of the Absolute* [*New Shelburne Essays,* vol. I] (Princeton: Princeton University Press, 1928), pp. 53–76, and "Marginalia, Part I," *American Review* VIII, 1 (Nov. 1936): 11–12.

15. More, "Modern Currents," p. 70.

16. Ibid.

17. Ibid., p. 71.

18. Ibid., p. 70.

19. Ibid., p. 71.

20. Ibid., pp. 71–72.

21. C. Hartley Grattan, ed., *The Critique of Humanism: A Symposium* (New York: Brewer and Warren Inc., 1930).

Sherwood, Stein, the Sentence, and Grape Sugar and Oranges

LINDA W. WAGNER

"There are some pretty wonderful sentences in it," Gertrude Stein writes to Sherwood Anderson in 1925, "and we know how fond we both are of sentences."[1] Stein's intimate confidence that Anderson will understand what she says about *The Making of Americans* surfaces again and again in her letters to him. The bond that existed between the two writers was that of craft; and for most writers, an understanding of their work creates the deepest kind of rapport. So well documented now in Ray Lewis White's *Sherwood Anderson/Gertrude Stein, Correspondence and Personal Essays,* the relationship between these two seminal American authors deserves more than the hasty cliché it has so often received in the past.

Anderson's admiration for Stein has long been a part of the Anderson myth. The anecdote of his brother Karl's bringing him a copy of *Tender Buttons,* trying to fathom the arresting qualities of the prose (when other readers were only laughing at it), has often been recounted. In fact, Anderson himself referred to it in his 1922 introduction to Stein's *Geography and Plays,* giving his brother there the important statement, " 'It gives words an oddly new intimate flavor and at the same time makes familiar words seem almost like strangers, doesn't it.' "[2]

Despite the fact that any writer is fascinated with words, Anderson's enthusiasm for *Tender Buttons* and Stein's later writing has been somewhat embarrassing for critics. If Anderson did admire Stein's words and sentences so fervently, why was there not more evidence of that admiration in his own prose? " 'There will be good sleighing,' said Will Henderson"[3] is hardly "Dining is west" or "Suppose ear rings, that is one way to breed, breed that."[4] Even David D. Anderson is forced to describe Stein's influence in highly general terms:

> The impact of the revolutionary nature of the Stein volume was so great that he remembered it all of his life as a revelation that he might be able to produce a style of his own . . .[5]

As sometimes happens in literary history, or in our subjective versions of it, even chronologists can err. Anderson did read *Tender Buttons,* but his introduction to Stein's writing was not that book but rather the 1909 *Three Lives* (as well as her two "portraits" of Henri Matisse and Pablo Picasso in Alfred Steiglitz's *Camera Work).*

The focus clears: edges sharpen, lines reach. In *Three Lives* Stein presents the prose portraits of three completely undistinguished women, Anna, Melanctha, and the gentle Lena (only Melanctha has now become distinguished, in her blackness). Working through simple words placed strangely in sentences, through sentences that refused to build to climactic (or even unclimactic) action, Stein created a montage of mood for each of these lives—unshakeable mood, giving the reader the emotional core of each life. Her disregard for ordinary plot, her evident love for the movement of the

words, her perverse choice of uninteresting characters—
here, in *Three Lives,* one genesis of Anderson's *Winesburg*
becomes a possibility.

To look more closely at Stein's *Lives* is to see that, even
here, each of the three stories has its own style, its own shape.
"The Good Anna" has as a basic note the refrain,

"You see that Anna led an arduous and troubled life."[6]
Written as a one-sentence paragraph, like so many of Stein's
objective but devastatingly clear sentences, this refrain appears regularly, early in the story, and then disappears as
Stein trusts the episodes of Anna's life to convey the same
literal meaning.

Most readers would find the unrelieved presentation of the
good Anna's unhappiness only depressing; Anderson, however, may have also been noticing Stein's methods of achieving her effects. "The Good Anna" is full of adjectives, many
of them linked in a chain of three or four, sometimes occur-
ring after the noun.

> Anna was all stiff, and inside all a quiver with shame,
> anxiety and grief. Even courageous Mrs. Lehntman, effi-
> cient, impulsive and complacent as she was and not deeply
> concerned in the event, felt awkward, abashed and almost
> guilty in that large, mild, helpless presence (p. 25).

These heavily descriptive sections create Stein's "mood,"
and in them her absorption in psychology, James, Bergson,
Whitehead—the whole psychic realism attempt—is clear.
No person is ever "simple"; no act can ever be "understood"
quickly. To suggest the basic anomaly of motivation, Stein
juxtaposes unlike adjectives. Instead of being repetitious, her
chains of modifiers often reflect the paradox she finds at the
heart of even the commonplace person. Anna was "all stiff
and inside all a quiver" Why not *yet* for *and?* Because Stein's
view of the situation is clearer; the description does not lend
itself to a simple dichotomy. Similar is the contradictory
alignment of the adjectives "efficient, impulsive and compla-

cent." It is true that not all the adjective chains are as dynamic as these, and some do repeat themselves, but quite often Stein launches multiple impressions with a series of very few words.

Contrasting with the mood passages, which are usually dominated by modifiers, are spare, objective statements. "Miss Mary Wadsmith was puzzled. She did not understand what Anna meant by what she said" (p. 25). These statements are frequently plot-oriented; at times they speak for the author. They not only change the swirling rhythm of the longer mood passages, they also keep the story moving in episodes. For example, this particular scene (in which the good Anna and her friend must tell Miss Mary, her employer, that she is leaving) opened with the two-paragraph sequence:

> It was very hard for the two women to begin.
> It must be very gently done, this telling to Miss Mary of the change (p. 25).

Rather than keeping her reader confused, as some of her ultradescriptive passages might, Stein seems intent on providing as much help for the reader as possible. She uses ample transitions; she creates moods as often as possible (important since each mood is integral to a characterization); and she uses refrain and imagery to sharpen the impressions she has created (her dogs sit "desolate in their corners like a lot of disappointed children whose stolen sugar has been taken from them").

Reading "The Good Anna," however, for all Stein's emphasis on clarity, is not like reading an O. Henry story. Part of the difference lies, as we have seen, in the incremental adjective use; part stems from her characteristic placing of adverbs and other modifiers after nouns ("Miss Mathilda *every day* put off the scolding. . . . When Miss Mathilda *early in the fall* came," pp. 11, 13); a larger part results from her use of balanced, almost periodic sentences, especially when those sentences come in clusters. Despite the fact that Stein does use some short sentences, most of her writing occurs in sentences like these two:

> Her voice was a pleasant one, when she told the histories of bad Peter and of Baby and of little Rags. Her voice was a high and piercing one when she called to the teamsters and to the other wicked men, what she wanted that should come to them, when she saw them beat a horse or kick a dog (p. 10).

Perfectly balanced, this pair reflects Stein's concern with what she called "the exactness of sense." As Fanny Butcher reminisces about Stein's awareness of the sentence,

> She talked with great enthusiasm about the evolution of the English language from the eighteenth century, when great writers all wrote sentences, their paragraphs merely composed of sentences. In the nineteenth century she said they thought in paragraphs, which are emotional, not intellectual units. She unconsciously was returning in her work to the sentence, she said, and she had written a long book on the subject . . .[7]

Stein's interest in the sentence as separate from the paragraph is apparent throughout her writing because she so often uses single-sentence paragraphs, thus calling attention to their separateness. The rigidly balanced sentence is also distinctive. Several other uses to which Stein puts the notion of sentence regularity are emphasis of sentence subject, and the creation of irony.

Throughout *Three Lives,* many consecutive sentences open with the same subject word, or its appropriate pronoun.

In "The Gentle Lena," five sentences (the five comprising one paragraph) open with either the word *Lena* or *She.*

> Lena was the second girl in her large family. She was at this time just seventeen years old. Lena was not an important daughter in the family. She was always sort of dreamy and not there. She worked hard and went very regularly at it, but even good work never seemed to bring her near (p. 159).

What is most interesting about this device is that such repetition seems to be Stein's rationale for paragraph division as well. The paragraph quoted is "about" Lena, and obviously so. The paragraph before this, however, opened with a sentence about a Mrs. Haydon; the one following concerns "Lena's age." Neither of these paragraphs has repetitive sentence subjects.

In using the balanced, regular sentence to create irony, Stein plays on the reader's grammatical expectations. We have noticed earlier her ironic use of *and;* she employs *and* between sentence elements as well, for a similar effect: "Melanctha went back to the hospital, and there the doctor told her she had the consumption" (p. 154). Part of the irony here occurs because in the previous paragraph Melanctha has been cured of a malady in the same hospital, so the reader is expecting that pattern rather than the simple futurity of the word *and.* A similar device is Stein's use of the appositive structure, as in "Melanctha never killed herself, she only got a bad fever . . ."

Increasingly throughout *Three Lives,* Stein uses expected grammatical structures for ironic effect. By the time of the third life, "The Gentle Lena," the very adjectives which introduce the patient German girl at the beginning of the story—"patient, gentle, sweet"—and those connected to the insensitive husband-to-be, Herman Kreder—"sullen and very good, and very quiet"—become Stein's refrain for the survivors after Lena's willed death, as Stein describes Herman as "very happy, very gentle, very quiet, very well content alone with his three children" (p. 181). From this use of her adjective sequence technique, Stein goes into many other kinds of verbal experimentation, but she never completely abandons the stylistic devices that were evident in *Three Lives.*

> I had already read a book of Miss Stein's called *Three Lives* and had thought it contained some of the best writing ever done by an American.[8]

The most immediate comparison to be made between Anderson's *Winesburg* stories and Stein's *Three Lives* is the subject matter. Undramatic, unwanted lives, for the most part— "grotesques" as Anderson called them, and by so doing, himself sabotaged the real applicability of his portraits— made vital only through their presentation. What had Stein, perhaps, contributed toward Anderson's presentation? Mood and incremental adjectives, figurative language, and refrain.

Mood:

> Snow lay deep in the streets of Winesburg. It had begun to snow about ten o'clock in the morning and a wind sprang up and blew the snow in clouds along Main Street. . . . "Snow will bring the people into town on Saturday. . . . Snow will be good for the wheat . . ."

In "The Teacher" Anderson creates a snow-bound isolation to introduce the isolation of both George Willard and Kate Swift, the teacher of the title. All the action occurs on the snowy night; all the emotions are bleak, and remain so: contact is never made. The central image—for the emotions of the characters as well as the story proper—occurs early:

> By nine o'clock of that evening snow lay deep in the streets and the weather had become bitter cold. It was difficult to walk about. The stores were dark and the people crawled away to their houses (p. #158).

Incremental adjectives, figurative language, refrain:

> Wing Biddlebaum talked much with his hands. The slender expressive fingers, forever active, forever striving to conceal themselves in his pockets or behind his back, came forth and became the piston rods of his machinery of expression (p. #28).

Seldom does Anderson combine this well, the graphic image with the figure of speech, but his fiction is full of attempts to do so. This passage is especially effective because it follows another good simile, "With a kind of wriggle, like a fish returned to the brook by a fisherman, Biddlebaum the silent began to talk . . . ," and leads to the succinct opening for the story proper: "The story of Wing Biddlebaum is a story of hands."

Instead of verbal refrain, Anderson uses images to create both character and mood: Wing's hands, Enoch Robinson's room, the chink in the glass window for the Rev. Hartman, Kate Swift's anger, Elizabeth Willard's make-up. By presenting the key to each emotional life graphically rather than rhetorically, Anderson gives his stories a sharp clarity that enables them to move quickly. The method provides an inherent condensation.

The places in which Anderson does use refrain are, instead, during dialogue between characters (more in the manner of Stein's technique in "Melanctha"). Elizabeth Willard's inarticulate gropings to reach her son contrast terribly with the passion of her plot to scissor her husband, if she must, to free the boy. All she manages to say is "I think you had better go out among the boys. You are too much indoors" (p. 48). (All Melanctha ever says is, "All I can do

82

now, Jeff, is to keep certainly with my believing you are good always, Jeff" (p. 104); unfortunately, Jeff has many more pages of convoluted rhetoric in his progress to understanding). Stein's rationale for her interest in repetition in dialogue/conversation fits logically with her attempt to present the precise attitude of each character, at each moment in question (speaking here about "Melanctha"):

> I began to get enormously interested in hearing how everybody said the same thing over and over again with infinite variations but over and over again until finally if you listened with great intensity you could hear it rise and fall and tell all that there was inside them, not so much by the actual words they said or the thoughts they had but by the movement of their thoughts and words endlessly the same and endlessly different.[9]

Repeatedly in the Winesburg stories, when the characters are in a position to reach each other, language fails them. Unrelieved, they turn away, all of them, even George Willard, saying his farewells to Helen White in "Sophistication."

> The boy's voice failed and in silence the two came back into town and went along the street to Helen White's house. At the gate he tried to say something impressive. Speeches he had thought out came into his head, but they seemed utterly pointless. "I thought—I used to think—I had it in my mind you would marry Seth Richmond. Now I know you won't," was all he could find to say as she went through the gate and toward the door of her house (p. 237).

It is this mood of isolation, of emotional poverty, that haunts the stories of *Winesburg* and gives them their strongest bond with Stein's *Three Lives.* When Anderson wrote that his interest in fiction was never in plot, but rather in "Human nature, the strange little whims, tragedies and comedies of

83

life itself,"[10] he was casting his lot with Stein's good Anna, Melanctha, and especially with the gentle Lena.

Stein's understated presentation of the inarticulate Lena's death, in what may be the most effective story of the three, caps her skill in shaping style to mood. "These were really bad days for poor Lena," she states in a cryptic short sentence; "Lena always was more and more lifeless and Herman now mostly never thought about her." The death of the marriage precedes Lena's physical death, and Stein's stolid monosyllabics perfectly reflect the dulling apathy: "When it was all over Lena had died, too, and nobody knew just how it had happened to her" (pp. 180–181).

Life as something "happening to" characters sets the mood as well for Anderson's equally exhausted protagonist in "Death in the Woods." One of his strongest stories, this account of old woman Grimes bears resemblances to Stein's Lena, and Anna, in that Mrs. Grimes was a bound girl, victimized in a German farmer's house, accepting marriage as the lesser of the all too prevalent evils. But the reality of her marriage, and her life, became so oppressive that her death by freezing was a simple relief.

Anderson's techniques in "Death in the Woods" are particularly Stein-like. His opening paragraph is marked by the sentence subject repetition that Stein used so effectively, with the added irony that all of the subjects are the word *She* rather than Mrs. Grimes's given name. So nondescript is Anderson's character that he does not ever mention her name.

> She was an old woman and lived on a farm near the town in which I lived. All country and small-town people have such old women, but no one knows much about them. Such an old woman comes into town driving an old worn-out horse or she comes afoot carrying a basket. She may own a few hens and have eggs to sell. She brings them in a basket and takes them to a grocer. There she trades

them in. She gets some salt pork and some beans. Then she gets a pound or two of sugar and some flour.[11]

The poignancy of the woman's nameless position in her culture is signaled further by Anderson's statement, "No one gave her a lift. People drive right down a road and never notice an old woman like that" (p. 533).

Anderson's key device in his presentation of the old woman is the use of refrain. "Then she settled down to feed stock. That was her job. . . . Every moment of every day, as a young girl, was spent feeding something" (p. 536). Bleak as this image of continuous physical labor is, the mood darkens when Anderson adds to it the threat of her husband's violence when she fails to keep everything fed—although he provides no means of feeding the stock—and the threat in her sexual relationship with him.

> Then she married Jake Grimes and he had to be fed. She was a slight thing, and when she had been married for three or four years, and after the two children were born, her slender shoulders became stooped (p. 537).

Had Anderson ended the story in the early years of the marriage, the similarities with Stein's Lena would be even more striking. But the story goes on, unrelieved, to prove repeatedly that the Grimes wife has exchanged her life of labor for one of abysmal, absurd struggle, to keep things alive even when her own life has become meaningless: "She had to scheme all her life about getting things fed" (537); "They left everything at home for her to manage and she had no money. She knew no one" (p. 538); and the crescendo to Anderson's use of the refrain,

> . . . Well, things had to be fed. Men had to be fed, and the horses that weren't any good but maybe could be

85

traded off, and the poor thin cow that hadn't given any milk for three months.

Horses, cows, pigs, dogs, men (p. 539).

In later sections of the story, Anderson juxtaposes the old woman's treatment at the hands of her family with her treatment by the apparently savage dogs. Brutalized as she had been by both her husband and her son, the old woman was yet saved from the violence that might have been expected from the dog pack by the animals themselves: "the dogs had not touched her body," Anderson reports with a Stein-like bluntness. His use of sentence variation to create the rhythms of the running dogs, and his use of parallel sentence structure[12] also suggest that Anderson is writing with more care than he often did.

That "Death in the Woods" is a more conscious, more introspective work than many of Anderson's stories is also clear because he frames the story with the author's involvement with the happening when he was only a boy. Fascinated with the mystically primitive scene—the woman's body young and beautiful in the snow—the writer has returned to the tale repeatedly as he himself has matured: "The notes had to be picked up slowly one at a time. Something had to be understood" (p. 548). In his gradual progress to understanding, Anderson again relied on the graphic, the concrete, the sensual, rather than the rhetorical, proving further that for him the essence of characterization lay in devices that reached deep into physical realities—tastes, colors, smells, touches.

His 1922 characterization of Stein herself is also full of graphic images (and adjectives) as he compares her with a bountiful, happy and decidedly American housewife, her "aroma" that of the fragrances of the kitchen. This passage from "Four American Impressions" is one small sample of the kind of understanding that existed between Stein and Anderson, major craftsmen and major humanists of twentieth century literature.

In my own boyhood in an Ohio town I went about delivering newspapers at kitchen doors, and there were certain houses to which I went—old brick houses with immense old-fashioned kitchens—in which I loved to linger. . . . Something got into my mind connected with the great light kitchens and the women working in them that came sharply back when, last year, I went to visit an American woman, Miss Gertrude Stein, in her own large room in the house at 27 rue de Fleurus in Paris. In the great kitchen of my fanciful world in which, ever since that morning, I have seen Miss Stein standing there is a most sweet and gracious aroma. Along the walls are many shining pots and pans, and there are innumerable jars of fruits, jellies and preserves. Something is going on in the great room, for Miss Stein is a worker in words with the same loving touch in her strong fingers that was characteristic of the women of the kitchens of the brick houses in the town of my boyhood. She is an American woman of the old sort, one who cares for the handmade goodies and who scorns the factory-made foods, and in her great kitchen she is making something with her materials, something sweet to the tongue and fragrant to the nostrils . . .

She is making new, strange and to my ears sweet combinations of words. As an American writer I admire her because she, in her person, represents something sweet and healthy in our American life, and because I have a kind of undying faith that what she is up to in her word kitchen in Paris is of more importance to writers of English than the work of many of our more easily understood and more widely accepted word artists.[13]

Anderson's stress on the Americanism of his friend illustrates his own loyalties to the country, and the region, that gave him what he consistently thought of as superior qualities; and his emphasis on the tactile, the sensual characteristics of Stein—both as writer and as person—is reminiscent of his devices in most of his best fiction.

And what of Stein? She was always very kind of Anderson,

praising him when she could (for his "directness," his vision), but realizing too that his skill in short fiction surpassed that in novels (and giving him reasons for his failures). But in her last published tribute to him, in 1942, Stein-the-teacher becomes simply Stein-the-friend, and her imagery here completes the aroma and taste of his earlier portrait of her.

Sherwood: Sweetness[14]

Yes undoubtedly, Sherwood Anderson had a sweetness, and sweetness is rare. Once or twice somebody is sweet, but everything in Sherwood was made of this sweetness. Here in war-time France they have made a new sugar, grape sugar, and it is as sweet as sugar and it has all through it the tang of a grape. That was Sherwood's sweetness, it was like that . . .

Funny I always connect Sherwood with sweet fruits. I remember in New Orleans when he came into the room he had a bag of oranges, twenty-five for twenty-five cents, and he and we ate all the twenty-five oranges; they were orange sweet, the kind that are twenty-five oranges for twenty-five cents way are orange sweet.

Dear Sherwood, as long as grape sugar is grape sugar and it always is, and oranges twenty-five for twenty-five cents are oranges, so long will Sherwood be Sherwood. And as grape sugar will always be, and oranges will always be, so will he.

One cannot cry when grape sugar is like that or twenty-five oranges for twenty-five cents are like that, and one cannot die when they are like that, so one does not cry for Sherwood nor does Sherwood die.

No.

Grape sugar and oranges twenty-five for twenty-five cents, they are Sherwood.

NOTES

1. Ray Lewis White, *Sherwood Anderson/Gertrude Stein, Correspondence and Personal Essays* (Chapel Hill: University of North Carolina Press, 1972), p. 49. Hereafter cited as White.

2. White, p. 15.

3. Sherwood Anderson, *Winesburg, Ohio* (New York: The Viking Press, 1964), p. 157.

4. Gertrude Stein, *Tender Buttons* (New York; Claire Marie, 1914), pp. 56, 28.

5. *Sherwood Anderson* (New York: Holt, Rinehart and Winston, 1967), p. 20. See also W. Sutton, *The Road to Winesburg*.

6. Gertrude Stein, *Three Lives* (London: Peter Owen, 1970), p. 10. Where possible, page numbers are included in text.

7. Fanny Butcher, *Many Lives—One Love* (New York: Harper and Row, 1972), p. 418.

8. White, p. 14. On p. 40, White quotes from Anderson's *A Story Teller's Story* in which he describes reading Stein as being a "sort of Lewis and Clark expedition."

9. Gertrude Stein, *Lectures in America* (Boston; Beacon Press, 1959), p. 138.

10. Quoted in Ray Lewis White, "A Critical Analysis," *Readers and Writers* I, No. 6 (Apr. 1968): p. 36.

11. "Death in the Woods," *The Portable Sherwood Anderson,* ed. Horace Gregory (New York: The Viking Press, 1949), p. 533.

12. From p. 542, *Portable,* "They began to play, running in circles in the clearing. Round and round they ran, each dog's nose at the tail of the next dog. In the clearing, under the snow-laden trees and under the wintry moon they made a strange picture, running thus silently, in a circle their running had beaten in the soft snow. The dogs made no sound. They ran around and around in the circle."
From p. 534, "The butcher in town, having been suddenly overcome with a feeling of pity, had loaded her grain bag heavily. It had been a big haul for the old woman.
It was a big haul for the dogs now."

13. "Four American Impressions" in *Sherwood Anderson's Notebook* (Mamaroneck, New York: Paul P. Appel, 1970), pp. 48–50.

14. White, pp. 114, 15, reprinted from *Story* XIX (Sept.-Oct. 1941): 63.

Anderson's Theories on Writing Fiction

MARTHA MULROY CURRY

Critics agree that Sherwood Anderson's enduring place in American literature rests upon his achievements in the short story rather than in the novel. Anderson's critical views regarding these two genres are the subject of this paper, but before beginning any discussion of what might be called Anderson's "critical views," two warnings must be given. First, we must remember that Anderson is primarily a creative artist, not a literary critic, and we must not expect from him precisely worded critical theories. More importantly, we must heed Anderson's own warning about his inability to state only the literal "truth." He admits in the Foreword to his fictionalized autobiography, *Tar: A Midwest Childhood:* "I have a confession to make. I am a story teller starting to tell a story and cannot be expected to tell the truth. Truth is impossible to me. It is like goodness, something aimed at but never hit."[1] In all his writing, what Anderson aims at achieving is not the literal "truth." As he tells us in his first autobiography, *A Story Teller's Story,* his aim is "to be true to the essence of things."[2]

The aim of this paper, too, is to arrive at the essence of

Anderson's critical thought regarding two specific genres, the short story and the novel. If we try to isolate statements from Anderson's nonfictional writing—his autobiographies, his letters, and his books of essays—we would surely distort the "truth" of his critical views. On the other hand, when we look at many of his statements in the context in which they are written, we can determine what Anderson thinks about the theoretical differences between the novel and the short story. We can also see what he says about the different ways in which he approaches the writing of the two genres. None of Anderson's statements presented in this paper are new. When these familiar statements, however, are used to illustrate his practice in some of his short stories and novels, we will be able to understand why he mastered the short story in a way he never mastered the novel.

Nowhere in Anderson's characteristically diffuse writings are there precise statements of critical thought. His *Writer's Book,* however, composed in the last decade of his life, can provide a focus for our study. In a letter to Maxwell Perkins in September 1938 Anderson indicates that he is organizing some of his essays into what he calls "a textbook for students" dealing with "the life of the writer, what difficulties the young writer has to face, what the real rewards are for the writer."[3] When Anderson died suddenly in 1941, he had not completely organized the essays. Furthermore, the essays are not standard textbook material. They are, rather, autobiographical and critical musings on the craft of writing and on Anderson's own experiences with both success and failure in the writing of short stories and novels. When Paul Rosenfeld brought out the first edition of Anderson's *Memoirs* in 1942, he included parts of three of the seven essays; but he changed, deleted, and transported passages at will. Ray Lewis White's critical edition of Anderson's *Memoirs,* published in 1969, correctly omits all of the *Writer's Book.* A critical edition of the *Writer's Book* in its entirety was published in 1975.[4] Two passages from this work will provide the organizational structure for our analysis of Anderson's critical theories regarding the short story and the novel. The first of the two passages is as follows:

> I have seldom written a story, long or short, that I did not have to write and rewrite. There are single short stories of mine that have taken me ten or twelve years to get written. It isn't that I have lingered over sentences . . .
>
> However, this has leaked through to me. There is the general notion, among those who make a business of literary criticism and who have done me the honor to follow me more or less closely in my efforts, that I am best at the short story.
>
> And I do not refer here to those who constantly come to me saying, *"Winesburg contains your best work,"* and who, when questioned, admit they have never read anything else. I refer instead to an opinion that is no doubt sound.
>
> The short story is the result of a sudden passionate interest. It is an idea grasped whole as one would pick an apple in an orchard. All of my own short stories have been written at one sitting, many of them under strange enough circumstances. There are these glorious moments, these pregnant hours, and I remember such hours as a man remembers the first kiss got from a woman loved (pp. 85–86).

No critic of Anderson would disagree with his judgment that *Winesburg, Ohio* is his "best work" or that he is "best at the short story." Critics also delight in the precision of the descriptive definition of the short story that is found in the passage "It is an idea grasped whole as one would pick an apple in an orchard." This definition inevitably reminds one of the beautiful *Winesburg* story "Paper Pills." The application of this definition to "Paper Pills" proves a remarkable congruence between Anderson's theory and practice in the short story.

The Table of Contents in *Winesburg, Ohio* tells us that

"Paper Pills" is a story "concerning Doctor Reefy." After introducing Doctor Reefy, whose "knuckles . . . were extraordinarily large . . . like clusters of unpainted balls as large as walnuts fastened together by steel rods," Anderson begins his story:

> The story of Doctor Reefy and his courtship of the tall dark girl who became his wife and left her money to him is a very curious story. It is delicious, like the twisted little apples that grow in the orchards of Winesburg. In the fall one walks in the orchards and the ground is hard with frost underfoot. The apples have been taken from the trees by the pickers. . . . On the trees are only a few gnarled apples that the pickers have rejected. They look like the knuckles of Doctor Reefy's hands. One nibbles at them and they are delicious. Into a little round place at the side of the apple has been gathered all of its sweetness. One runs from tree to tree over the frosted ground picking the gnarled, twisted apples and filling his pockets with them. Only the few know the sweetness of the twisted apples.[5]

Just as Doctor Reefy, and actually all of the "grotesques" who live in Winesburg, are epitomized by their likeness to the twisted little apples, so Anderson epitomizes the short story by the same figure of an apple. Just as an apple is an organic whole, so a short story must be an organic, living whole. One can imagine Sherwood Anderson as a boy running through the apple orchards near Clyde, Ohio, and picking the gnarled and twisted apples, recognizing that in the gnarled place at the side of the apples all the sweetness resides. After reading his mature stories, the reader also realizes that in Anderson's gnarled, twisted people there is a place where all the sweetness is gathered. As he wrote to Mary Helen Dinsmoor in 1938: "It seemed to me that I had found some spot of beauty in each of them."[6] The short story is an idea grasped whole; the short story by Sherwood An-

derson is usually an idea about the hidden beauty and sweetness twisted into a form called "grotesque" by the indifferent
and unsympathetic.

Anderson also expresses the belief that the short story is
an organic whole when he uses the metaphor of certain
words or actions being "seeds" impregnating his imagination. This metaphor occurs frequently in Anderson's works,
and is most fully developed in *A Story Teller's Story:* "People
constantly told me tales. . . . A few such sentences . . . were
the seeds of stories. How could one make them grow?" (p.
255) In the *Writer's Book,* after saying that "the short story
is the result of a sudden passionate interest," Anderson continues: "There are these glorious moments, these pregnant
hours." The remaining pages of the *Writer's Book* are a
detailed explanation of three such "moments," such
"hours." Before we examine the statements made in these
pages, let us consider the other description in the *Writer's
Book* of Anderson's method of writing the short story: "The
writing of the short story is a kind of explosion" (p. 80).

It is interesting to hear Anderson using the same word
"explosion" at least ten years earlier. In a letter to Marietta
Finley Hahn, written on December 18, 1924, Anderson describes what must have been a characteristic manner of writing: "When the nerves are tired from long thinking and
feeling there comes often a kind of explosion. A hundred
images come—stories tales poems. None of them complete
the circle. They break off and disappear."[7] Even earlier, at
the time of the publication of *Winesburg, Ohio* and when he
was working on a group of stories that he hoped to publish
as a novel called "Mary Cochran," Anderson writes to
Winesburg's publisher, Benjamin Huebsch: "These individual tales come clear and sharp. When I am ready for one of
them it comes all at one sitting, a distillation, an outbreak."[8]

The second passage from the *Writer's Book* that serves to
organize this paper opens with Anderson's description of the
writing of the short story as a "kind of explosion" and ends

with a statement that saddens all lovers of Anderson's stories. The complete passage is as follows:

> The writing of the short story is a kind of explosion. I think it was Mr. H. G. Wells who once described the writing of the short story by the figure of a man running to a fire and the novel by the figure of the same man taking an afternoon stroll.
>
> But it is not as simple as that. A man writes a novel as he takes an afternoon stroll only in his imagination. The actual physical feat of writing either a long or a short novel is another matter.
>
> There is his theme and he must hang on to it day after day, month after month and often year after year. He must carry the theme within himself in all the changing circumstances of a life. There will be, during the process of the writing, birth and death. He must perhaps move from place to place . . .
>
> The man is constantly swept by all sorts of emotions having nothing to do with the work in hand. Some minor character in his novel begins suddenly to run away with his book. He is like a general, trying to manage a vast army during a battle. It is not enough that he has made the characters in his novel seem alive and real to us. He must think his way through their relations to each other. He must orchestrate his work, give it what is called "form." It is not for nothing that we honor the novelist above the simple story tellers. The novel is the real test of the man. (pp. 80–81).

The two similes which he attributes to H. G. Wells[9] provide Anderson with a vivid and dramatic comparison between the writing of the short story and the writing of the novel. In describing "the writing of the short story by the figure of a man running to a fire and the novel by the figure of the same man taking an afternoon stroll," Anderson shows that he shares with his contemporaries the prevailing

95

attitude toward both the short story and the novel. Even though Anderson implies that taking an afternoon stroll is easier than running to a fire, it would seem that for Anderson it is easier, it is more exciting and stimulating, to run to a fire than to walk all afternoon, even at a leisurely pace. Perhaps Anderson would have lost interest and not have sustained the discipline needed to complete a well-planned walk to a predetermined destination. Although Anderson may have found it easier to run to a fire than to take an afternoon stroll, why should he depreciate running to the fire? In the terms of the simile, even granted that in the last analysis more energy is expended in taking an afternoon walk than in running to a fire, is it better to take the afternoon walk? In the terms of Anderson's literary context, an important critical question is raised: granted that more time is consumed and energy expended in writing the novel than the short story, is the novel thereby a better work of art?

Anderson's answer is the usual one for his day: "It is not for nothing that we honor the novelist above the simple story tellers. The novel is the real test of the man." Readers, publishers, and critics all expected serious fiction writers to produce novels, not volumes of short stories. Furthermore, novels sold, but collections of short stories did not. People who were buying books during Anderson's life never would have heeded Horace Gregory's warning: "One never measures Anderson's writings by their physical size."[10] Since, after 1922 when he definitively left his advertising job in Chicago, Anderson had to live by his pen, he persisted, despite his better inclinations, to write full-length novels. Therefore, in the passage from the *Writer's Book* under consideration, Anderson feels obliged to explain the reasons why the writing of the novel is more difficult than the writing of the short story. The three problems Anderson singles out—theme, character, and form—are three of the basic problems that beset Anderson whenever he attempted to write novels.

Anderson begins his discussion of the novelist and "the actual physical feat of writing either a long or a short novel" with a discussion of the difficulty of sustaining a theme. The passage is also a remarkably close description of several periods in Anderson's life, especially of the time he was trying to write his early novels in Elyria, Ohio. "There is his theme and he must hang on to it day after day, month after month and often year after year. He must carry the theme within himself in all the changing circumstances of a life. There will be, during the process of the writing, birth and death. He must move from place to place. He suddenly finds for himself a new woman, begins to want her. He is a poor man and must, in some way, manage to make a living." It was during the Elyria years that both his first marriage and his business career were showing the strain placed upon them by his attempts to do significant creative writing, and Anderson brought several novels with him when he returned to Chicago from Elyria in 1913. Two of these novels subsequently were published, *Windy McPherson's Son* and *Marching Men*. In neither of them is one central theme consistently maintained and developed.

Let us take as our example *Windy McPherson's Son*, the story of Sam McPherson. After an early life of ineffectual wanderings Sam McPherson settles in Chicago and becomes a successful businessman, successful, that is, in monetary terms but unsuccessful in achieving a life of meaning and beauty. It is not difficult for the reader who is familiar with the details of Anderson's life to see a great deal of Sherwood, to say nothing of his father, Irwin McLain Anderson, in Windy and his son Sam. *Windy McPherson's Son,* however, was not intended to be a loose, rambling, fictionalized autobiography, as was *Tar.* Reading the novel convinces one that it was intended to be a novel whose thematic center is the initiation of a youth into meaningful adult life. Anderson could not, however, sustain this theme. At the end of the novel, when Sam returns to his wife after some more years of aimless wandering, he brings three orphan children for her to raise. In a book containing numerous novelistic faults, this ending was the one thing that Anderson decided to change when a second edition was published by Ben Huebsch in 1921. Anderson writes to Huebsch in November 1921, about the book: "All the later part of it represents too much my own flounderings about in life." Therefore, in an attempt to find a suitable ending, Anderson says: "My mind reached back into childhood."[11] Nonetheless, when the revised edition was published, nothing substantial was changed. The ending remains inconclusive.

The letter to Huebsch gives some of the reasons why *Windy McPherson's Son* does not succeed as a novel—"the crudities of the book, the occasionally terrible sentences, the minor faults"[12]; it also explains why some of the short stories written but a few years after *Windy* did succeed. The key words in the letter are "flounderings" and "my mind reached back into childhood." In the years between 1915 and 1917 Anderson wrote the *Winesburg* stories in a rooming house on Chicago's Near North side. At this time, in a work composed of individual tales, Anderson could utilize his flounderings and questionings about the meaning of his youthful years in Clyde and the thwarted people he knew there.

In the passage from the *Writer's Book* that we are using as a framework for this investigation of Anderson's difficulties in the writing of novels, after speaking about the difficulty of sustaining his theme, Anderson turns to the problem of characterization. "Some minor character in his novel begins suddenly to run away with his book. He is like a general, trying to manage a vast army during a battle. It is not enough that he has made the characters in his novel seem alive and real to us. He must think his way through their relations to each other" (p. 81). Anderson could make his characters "come alive" but he could not always "think his way through their relations to each other." A good example of this limitation is his novel *Poor White*, published in 1920. Although many critics consider *Poor White* Anderson's most successful novel, it, too, is marred by his failure to integrate all of his admittedly vivid characters into one plot and theme.[13]

Anderson admits, both in his Introduction to the 1926 Modern Library edition of the novel and when in his *Memoirs* he discusses his aim in writing it, that *Poor White* is the story of Bidwell, Ohio, rather than the story of Hugh McVey and the other characters who impinge upon his life. The greatest novels, however, are not stories of towns but stories of human beings. Anderson, of course, knows this. Is it mere disingenuousness that Anderson ends his Introduction to the Modern Library edition in this way: "I wish 'Poor White' were better done. The book is, however, far from me. It is no longer mine. And when it comes to that, I wish all books were better done. They will never be too well done—at least not by me."[14]

The last difficulty that Anderson mentions regarding his inability to master the writing of novels relates to the question of form. Anderson knows that the novelist "must orchestrate his work, give it what is called 'form.' " As early as 1921 Anderson writes to Paul Rosenfeld about this concern. In a review of *Poor White* in the *New Republic* in November 1920, Francis Hackett, although he concedes that Anderson "is able to breathe life into his characters," criticizes his "small sense of the values of form." In the final analysis, however, Hackett claims that in *Poor White* Anderson could "produce a curious large illusion of life."[15] Hackett's review is obviously in the back of Anderson's mind when he writes to Rosenfeld in March 1921:

I wonder about your strictures regarding form. Is it inevitable that the matter of form become uppermost in the critic's mind? Must he always have that ground to stand on? . . .

Hackett always attacks me by saying my sense of form is atrocious, and it may be true. However, he also commends me for getting a certain large, loose sense of life. I often wonder, if I wrapped my packages up more neatly, if the same large, loose sense of life could be attained.[16]

Thus, Anderson realizes that his forte is in achieving this "large, loose sense of life." Nonetheless, various statements that he makes in the 1920s and 1930s indicate that his difficulties in imposing form on his novels is related to his difficulties with characterization.

He writes to his good friend Jerome Blum in 1926, telling him about a new novel he alternatively called "Another Man's House" or "Other People's Houses." He tells Blum: "It's the old business of trying to get too much into one book and getting it messed up. The simple direct form of the thing only seems to emerge for me after a lot a sweating. I put doodads all over the house and then have to go around and knock them off." Almost ten years later, on November 8, 1935, he writes to Maxwell Perkins, remarking that a friend has told him that the canvases of his novels are too crowded, particularly too crowded with characters. Anderson accepts this criticism, as well as the criticism that he has difficulty imposing a clearly defined form on his novels: "I have, almost always, tried to work out of pure feeling, having the conviction that if I got the feeling straight and pure enough, the form I wanted would follow. I am trying to make this job more objective, keep the whole story definitely on two or three people, . . . trying, you see, to use mind as well as feeling."[17]

Finally, in a late critical essay entitled "Man and His Imagination" Anderson comments on his last novel, *Kit Brandon,* published in 1936. In the context of explaining the relation between reality and fiction, he describes how he creates his fictional characters. A woman rumrunner he came to know when he was covering bootlegging trials in rural Virginia became the "seed" for the fictional woman who gave her name to the novel. It was only when he fully transformed the actual rumrunner into his fictional character that the novel *Kit Brandon* "came alive" with its own form and substance:

What I am trying to say is that the new woman, the central figure, in my story no longer lived in the reality of her own life, but that she had a new life in this imaginative world. This is a matter that is a little difficult sometimes to make people understand who are not writers. A book or story that comes alive, that really has form and substance, has its own life and it is right here that violence is so often done to the art of writing.[18]

Critics of Anderson, however, still have difficulty in determining exactly what he means when he uses the word "form." How can we extract the "essence" of what he means? Even though Anderson, when speaking of form, uses verbal ploys such as "that was a quite different matter," perhaps the following quotations will enable us finally to distill the essence of his meaning. Reference has already been made to the section of *A Story Teller's Story* where Anderson uses the metaphor of a pregnant woman to explain his method of creating stories. The same section is also a condemnation of what Anderson calls the plot stories, plot novels, and plot plays that reduce much of the creative literature in America to a commercialized and standardized mediocrity. Anderson writes that, in order to remedy the situation:

What was wanted I thought was form, not plot, an altogether more elusive and difficult thing to come at.

In certain moods one became impregnated with the seeds of a hundred new tales in one day. The telling of the tales, to get them into form, to clothe them, find the words and the arrangement of words that would clothe them—that was a quite different matter.

The words used by the tale teller were as the colors used by the painter. Form was another matter. It grew out of the materials of the tale and the teller's reaction to them.

It was the tale trying to take form that kicked about inside the tale teller at night when he wanted to sleep.[19]

These quotations from *A Story Teller's Story* remind one of the first story in *Winesburg, Ohio,* "The Book of the Grotesque." This story serves as an introduction to the whole of *Winesburg,* and Anderson's imaginative conception of the old writer in the story gives form to all of the subsequent stories as well as to the book as a whole. The old writer "was like a pregnant woman," and as he lay in his bed at night "figures began to appear before his eyes. He imagined the young indescribable thing within himself was driving a long procession of figures before his eyes. . . . They were all grotesques." Each figure that the writer imagined had been turned into a grotesque because he had "snatched up" one of the many beautiful truths that were in the world, "called it his truth, and tried to live his life by it."[20] The old writer was then compelled to get out of bed and write down the stories of the grotesques. These stories are, of course, *Winesburg, Ohio.*

Therefore, although a highly novelistic form and complete integration of characters into one unified novel are difficult, if not impossible, for Anderson to achieve, in his short stories he was able to achieve consummate form. This should not surprise us. When, in the *Writer's Book* of the late 1930s, Anderson describes the circumstances in which he writes his short stories, he says: "I am trying to sing in these words put down here the more glorious moments in a writer's life" (p. 88). A few pages later he adds: "I am trying, as I have said, to give an impression of moments that bring glory into the life of the writer" (p. 91). The "more glorious moments," the moments that bring true glory to Anderson as a writer, are the moments in which he writes his shorter works. Let us, therefore, look at what he tells us about the way he writes his stories.

First, he explains: "It isn't that I have lingered over sentences" (p. 85). Earlier in the *Writer's Book* Anderson says:

"I have never been one who can correct, fill in, rework his stories" (p. 28). In his *Memoirs* Anderson makes the same claim. He says that "I'm a Fool" is "one of the stories that never had to be retouched, no word, comma, period ever changed"; and of "Hands" he says: "The story was written that night in one sitting. No word of it ever changed."[21] Although other statements in Anderson's published and unpublished writings, and in particular, the manuscripts of his works housed in the Newberry Library in Chicago, prove that he often changed words, commas, periods, and, in fact, whole sentences in his works, the statements quoted from his *Memoirs* are substantially correct, even if false when taken too literally. Although Anderson did make numerous relatively minor changes in his manuscripts, by temperament he was not inclined to "correct, fill in, rework" the details of his stories. Evidence for this fact is also provided by the vast manuscript collection at the Newberry Library.

Instead of reworking a story or a section of a book, Anderson often rewrote it completely. "I must try and when I fail must throw away" (p. 28). Later in the *Writer's Book* he gives the following advice to the young writer whom he is addressing: "A man should write and throw away. Write and throw away again" (p. 84). His letter indicates that such, indeed, was his practice in all his works, long as well as short. Anderson writes to Gertrude Stein from Reno in the spring of 1923, when he was working on *A Story Teller's Story:* "It has been a job. So much to discard. Have never thrown away so much stuff."[22] In the summer of 1925 Anderson was writing *Tar* in the mountains of southwest Virginia. *The Woman's Home Companion* had agreed to give it serial publication prior to its publication in book form. In a letter to one of the editors of the magazine, written in July 1925, Anderson speaks of the difficulty he is having with the book: "I have worked on it all summer and thrown away all I have written." In September he writes in much the same vein to his literary agent Otto Liveright: "During the month up in the country I wrote about 50,000 words on the Childhood book but threw away about half of it when I came home as not quite up to what I wanted." Nevertheless, he can tell Liveright: "It keeps going along."

If Anderson's habitual practice is to "write and throw away," the key passage from the *Writer's Book* that describes the "glorious moments" when he writes his short stories also provides another important insight into his method of creation. As we know, the passage begins: "I have seldom written a story, long or short, that I did not have to write and rewrite. There are single short stories of mine that have taken me ten or twelve years to get written. It isn't that I have lingered over sentences . . ." Earlier in the same work Anderson remarks: "Some of my best stories have been written ten or twelve times, and there is one story, 'Death in the Woods,' a magnificent tale, one of the most penetrating written in our times, that was ten years getting itself written" (p. 28).

It is not surprising that an author who believes that a short story is "an idea grasped whole" sometimes needs ten or twelve years in which to write a story, nor that he has to rewrite and rewrite the story ten or twelve times. The passive voice used by Anderson in these passages is instructive. The writer does not actually take ten or twelve years to write a story, but the story sometimes takes "ten or twelve years to get written." Furthermore, the idea for the story sometimes takes ten years to be "grasped whole." Since Anderson says that "Death in the Woods" was ten years "getting itself written," we can use it as an example of Anderson's method of writing his stories.

With the Anderson Papers in the Newberry Library is a twenty-two-page manuscript entitled "Death in the Forest."[23] The story describes the death of "Ma Marvin," which occurred in the middle of "grimes woods" on a snowy night in December. Attached to the manuscript is a note in Mrs. Eleanor Anderson's hand: "Early version of short story Death in the Woods." A greatly revised version was published in the *American Mercury* in September of the same year. Anderson's last volume of collected short stories, *Death in the Woods,* published in 1933, opens with this story. Since the version that appeared in *American Mercury* in 1926 is virtually the same story as it appears in the 1933 volume of collected stories, we can assume that the original version was written about 1916, when Anderson was writing the final versions of his Winesburg tales.

Evidence shows that, in fact, Anderson was still trying to write the story to his satisfaction when he was living in Palos Park, Illinois, between 1920 and 1922. Even though, as related in *Tar,* the first suggestion for the story came to Anderson from a childhood experience and in the account in *Tar* there is no mention of the half-savage dogs, in his *Memoirs* Anderson tells us that the first "impulse" for the story came to him one time in Palos Park when he, on a snowy, moonlit night, watched a pack of dogs running in a circle around him as he lay stretched out on a log in a clearing: "It was on that night I got the impulse for one of my best stories, the title story for the volume *Death in the Woods.* I did not succeed in writing it at once. It was one of the stories I wrote, threw away and rewrote many times."[24]

The next development in the creation of the story is revealed to us in *A Story Teller's Story.* As Anderson is working on this autobiography in Reno in 1923 he is still striving to combine the idea of the old woman dying in the forest with the idea of the half-wild dogs running in a circle around a solitary figure on a cold wintry night. The passage from *A Story Teller's Story* also shows that only in grasping whole the germinal idea behind a story can Anderson truly organize and give form to his story:

> And what a world that fanciful one—how grotesque, how strange, how teeming with strange life! Could one ever bring order into that world? In my own actual work as a tale teller I have been able to organize and tell but a few of the fancies that have come to me. There is a world into which no one but myself has ever entered and I would like to take you there, but how often when I go, filled with

confidence, to the very door leading into that strange world, I find it locked. Now, in the morning, I myself cannot enter the land into which all last night, as I lay awake in my bed, I went alone at will.

There are so many people in that land of whom I should like to tell you. I should like to take you with me through the gate into the land, let you wander there with me. There are people there with whom I should like you to talk. There is the old woman accompanied by the gigantic dogs who died alone in a wood on a winter day . . .[25]

Thus, shortly before he published "Death in the Woods" in *American Mercury* in 1926, he was able to give definitive form to the story of the death of Ma Grimes.

When an idea finally has been "grasped whole," when the story is finally ready "to get written," Anderson could often in a final burst of creative energy write the story "at one sitting." Although Anderson most certainly stretches the literal truth when he claims, as he does in the *Writer's Book,* that "all of my own short stories have been written at one sitting," we reach the essential truth of his method of creating stories when we realize that the story, in all of its details and in its definitive form, is written in one glorious moment of inspiration.

Have we now arrived at the point where we are able to summarize Anderson's theories regarding the writing of the novel and the short story? We have already seen that Anderson, after giving two striking similes for writing the short story and the novel—describing "the writing of the short story by the figure of a man running to a fire and the novel by the figure of the same man taking an afternoon stroll"— makes the statement: "But it is not as simple as that. A man writes a novel as he takes an afternoon stroll only in his imagination. The actual physical feat of writing either a long or a short novel is another matter" (p. 80). Here Anderson performs one of his characteristic sleights of his pen. Just when the reader is expecting him to reveal something definite regarding his critical stance, Anderson slips out from under his scrutiny. Later in the *Writer's Book,* after describing the circumstances in which he wrote an unnamed story in a train station in Harrodsburg, Kentucky, and the story "I'm a Fool" in his Chicago advertising office, and before he starts to describe the writing of "The Man's Story" in Stark Young's apartment in New York, Anderson admits: "I am, to be sure, speaking only of the writing of short stories. The writing of the long story, the novel, is another matter. I had intended, when I began to write, to speak of the great gulf that separates the two arts, but I have been carried away by this remembering of the glorious times in the life of the writer of short tales" (p. 89). The last of these characteristically vague remarks comes toward the end of his description of writing "The Man's Story": "I had started here to speak of the relationship of the story to the novel but have been carried away" (p. 91).

Yes, when Anderson starts to become specific about a theoretical distinction he soon is "carried away" or, actually, carried back into a more congenial manner of writing. In the *Writer's Book,* as in his major work of his last years, his *Memoirs,* Anderson returns to the fragmentary and episodic form that he has mastered. If Anderson cannot translate into theory what he instinctively understands and practices as an artist, neither he nor his reader should be disappointed. Even though his novels are flawed, Anderson knows he has his "glorious moments" of inspiration, and nothing can deprive him or his reader of some of the finest short stories written in English in our century.

NOTES

1. Edited by Ray Lewis White (Cleveland: Case Western Reserve University Press, 1969), p. 5.
2. Edited by Ray Lewis White, (Cleveland: Case Western Reserve University Press, 1968), p. 76.
3. Outgoing letters, Newberry Library, 1938; published in *Letters of Sherwood Anderson,* edited by Jones and Rideout, p. 411. All letters

quoted in the text are with the Anderson Papers at the Newberry Library. If they are also published in the Jones and Rideout edition, the page number of this edition will be given. If they are only in manuscript at the Newberry Library, they will simply be identified in the text.

4. Martha Mulroy Curry, The "Writer's Book" by Sherwood Anderson: A Critical Edition (Metuchen, N.J.: The Scarecrow Press, 1975); page numbers for quotations from this work will be given in parentheses in the text. Ray Lewis White explains on p. xxxiv of his Introduction to Sherwood Anderson's Memoirs: A Critical Edition his reasons for excluding the Writer's Book.

5. New York: B. W. Huebsch, 1919, pp. 18 and 19–20.

6. Letter of August 1938, as quoted in "An Inquiry into the Life of Sherwood Anderson as Reflected in His Literary Works" (unpublished M.A. thesis, Ohio University, 1939), p. 53.

7. Anderson Papers, Newberry Library, reserved box 7: Mrs. Hahn's letters from Sherwood Andersoon; quoted in Sutton, The Road to Winesburg, p. 230.

8. When manuscript letters are quoted, Anderson's spelling and punctuation are standardized.

9. Anderson is not quoting Wells exactly; however, in Experiments in Autobiography (New York: Macmillan Company, 1934), p. 532, Wells says: "I write as I walk because I want to get somewhere and I write as straight as I can, just as I walk as straight as I can, because that is the best way to get there."

10. "Editor's Introduction," The Portable Sherwood Anderson, p. 15.

11. Letters, edited by Jones and Rideout, pp. 81 and 82.

12. Letters, edited by Jones and Rideout, p. 82.

13. Critics who regard Poor White as Anderson's best novel include: Howe, Sherwood Anderson, p. 123; Brom Weber, Sherwood Anderson (Minneapolis: University of Minesota Press, 1964), p. 32; and Frederick Hoffman, "The Voices of Sherwood Anderson," Shenandoah 13 (Spring 1962): 5–19. Nathan Bryllion Fagin, The Phenomenon of Sherwood Anderson (Baltimore: The Rossi-Bryn Company, 1927), pp. 40–41, and David D. Anderson, Sherwood Anderson: An Introduction and Interpretation, p. 60, point out that poor characterization weakens Poor White.

14. New York: Viking Press, 1926, p. viii.

15. 24 (Nov. 24, 1920), p. 330

16. Letters, edited by Jones and Rideout, pp. 71–72.

17. Ibid., p. 331.

18. Published in The Intent of the Artist, edited by Augusto Centeno (Princeton: Princeton University Press, 1941), p. 57.

19. A Story Teller's Story, edited by Ray Lewis White, pp. 255, 257, and 261.

20. Ibid., pp. 2–5

21. Ibid., pp. 433 and 352. William L. Phillips' "How Sherwood Ander-

son Wrote *Winesburg, Ohio,"American Literature,* 23 (Mar. 1951): 7–30, and his "Sherwood Anderson's *Winesburg, Ohio:* Its Origins, Composition, Technique, and Reception" (doctoral dissertation, University of Chicago, 1949) are excellent studies of the manuscript of Winesburg.

22. *Letters,* edited by Jones and Rideout, p. 95.

23. The Appendix to William Vaughn Miller's "The Technique of Sherwood Anderson's Short Stories" (doctoral dissertation, University of Illinois, 1969), prints the manuscript, pp. 259–68. Pages 245–46 describe the published versions of "Death in the Woods."

24. Sherwood Anderson's *Memoirs,* p. 425.

25. *A Story Teller's Story,* p. 92.

Anderson's Letters
to Marietta D. Finley Hahn:
A Literary Chronicle

WILLIAM A. SUTTON

Between September 26, 1916, and an unspecified day in April 1933, Sherwood Anderson wrote 308 letters to Marietta D. Finley, of Indianapolis, who, in 1928, became the wife of Dr. E. Vernon Hahn, also of Indianapolis. Anderson had met Marietta, known as Bab, in Chicago in the fall of 1914 through a friend whom she was visiting, and their mutual attraction resulted in their long-time correspondence, of which, unfortunately, only half survives.

When the Newberry Library, upon being designated by Mrs. Eleanor Copenhaver Anderson as the repository for his papers, began a systematic collection of Anderson's letters, Mrs. Hahn's name was on its list of prospects. Dr. Stanley Pargellis, then the director of the Newberry Library, wrote to Mrs. Hahn in 1947, asking her, as was customary, to donate her letters to the Anderson Collection. She replied that, in view of the considerable financial help she had rendered to Anderson and members of his family, she thought a payment of $8,000 would be appropriate. The library was in no position to offer such a sum.

In 1962 I became aware of Mrs. Hahn through the presence of her name in the Newberry's Development File, the list of people from whom the library hoped to make acquisitions. At the time, I was working on *The Road to Winesburg* (published in 1972), on which I had begun work in 1941 when I wrote my doctoral dissertation at the Ohio State University on Anderson's early life. Because Mrs. Hahn's home in Indianapolis was only sixty miles from mine in Muncie, it seemed necessary that I should become acquainted with a prime Anderson source so close to home.

The library had an old address for Mrs. Hahn. After one letter was returned, I made an appeal to medical friends, who approached the matter through Dr. Hahn's address in a medical directory. Dr. Hahn had died, but my friends did produce an address for Mrs. Hahn, who was living in a cooperative housing unit, The Propylaeum, in Indianapolis. She was then seventy-three years of age and recuperating from a very serious illness.

After receiving permission to visit Mrs. Hahn and making an appropriate appointment, I was greeted, upon entering Mrs. Hahn's one-room apartment with these words: "Why did Sherwood Anderson marry Tennessee Mitchell?" Eventually, it became clear that she was still regretting that, when Sherwood's marriage to Cornelia Lane Anderson failed, he had married Tennessee Mitchell instead of her.

Later, after she had made the letters available, one question which I asked was, "Why, in view of the beginning of the relationship in the fall of 1914, is the first letter written by Anderson dated September 26, 1916?" Mrs. Hahn's answer to this was, "He did write me letters before that, but he asked me to destroy them. Like a fool, I did." As readers of the letters will see, they amply suggest Miss Finley's intense interest in Anderson and his successful effort to make her think of her life in terms independent of his own.

Although the Newberry Library files had supplied the information that Mrs. Hahn had an undetermined number of letters, during my first visit no mention of letters was made. Not long after various comments about Anderson had been made, Mrs. Hahn pleased me by exclaiming, "You *do* know something about Anderson!" Then she mentioned, quite casually, that she owned the manuscript of *Marching Men*. This revelation was a complete surprise and a matter of great excitement to me as an Anderson biographer. I asked whether it might be seen. Mrs. Hahn replied that she could get it out of storage and that another appointment might be made to examine it.

This appointment was made. I found Mrs. Hahn a truly delightful person, so much so that I took my wife with me on the next visit. At that time Mrs. Hahn mentioned that she had the manuscript ready and proceeded to lay a bed sheet on the rug. Puzzled, I asked why she was doing that. She said, "Oh, when you handle it, it flakes so." Astounded, I begged Mrs. Hahn not to handle it further, to leave it in a large brown envelope that contained it, and I did not then examine it.

In the ensuing discussion, I urged Mrs. Hahn to put the novel, which was basically written on news copy paper, then about fifty years brittle, into a place where it could be preserved. She remarked that she had thought of placing it in the Lilly Collection at Indiana University. I pointed out that the Newberry had the Anderson Collection but agreed that good care would be given at Indiana University or any other adequate library.

Shortly after we talked of the *Marching Men* manuscript, Mrs. Hahn mentioned the letters she had. I feigned surprise and then asked whether they might be examined. Presumably taking a certain impish pleasure, she said, "Your copy is on the table beside you." In a package, about four inches thick, was the carbon of a typescript which Mrs. Hahn explained she, a trained typist, had made when she and her husband, a neurosurgeon and psychiatrist, were thinking of doing a "psychiatric biography" of Anderson. The letters proved to be exciting.

In this period, I was spending much time working at Newberry Library. One Friday I arrived in Muncie for the weekend and found a letter from Mrs. Hahn which stated she had decided that, as soon as she could get out to the post office, she was going to mail the letters and the *Marching Men* manuscript to the Newberry, thus following my suggestion to place them there.

Much disturbed over the idea of the crumbling manuscript going through the mail, I called Mrs. Hahn and volunteered to provide personal transportation of the treasure to Chicago. She readily agreed, and the next day I visited her to get the items, which filled a suitcase. Included was a previously unmentioned manuscript of Anderson's "Seeds." Also, it turned out that there were 308 letters instead of the 256 in the typescript.

When Mrs. Hahn put the manuscript material in my hands, she said she wanted some payment. She did not want to realize on them in a commercial way, for she could have gained much more by auctioning them and she knew it. Further, for a long time she had been quite independent financially, before as well as after her marriage. She did, however, want the Newberry to make a contribution.

Then I expressed a willingness to act as her agent in the matter. To this she readily agreed. Without discussing the matter with her, I decided that the Newberry ought to offer, getting a great bargain, $1,000 and an expert appraisal for tax purposes.

Thus, the next Monday, I informed James Wells, the appropriate member of the library staff, that Mrs. Hahn wanted to place her Anderson holdings in the library, that she wanted payment, and invited an offer. Later that day, he informed me that the library was willing to offer $1,000. Marveling at the coincidence of the offer and amount in his mind, I got ready acceptance of the idea of the expert's appraisal. A few hours thereafter, the precious Anderson material was delivered to Wells's office.

Before all this happened, I had been shown by Dr. Pargellis two Anderson letters of no particular distinction, which had just been bought for $35. Thus, it was apparent that the entire package, at that time, would be thought of as worth approximately $10,000. The expert appraiser placed a value of $4,500 on the documents.

I found several of the letters of great value in preparing *The Road to Winesburg,* which Anderson students will note contains the letter written during Anderson's amnesia attack in Elyria in 1912. Neither Schevill nor Howe had been allowed to reprint it, though they knew of it and alluded to it. Thus I suggested to Mrs. Eleanor Anderson that it was time to reproduce this most revealing and unique document. She demurred, saying that Sherwood had not had amnesia, that he had told her he had only been pretending to have amnesia.

The letter Anderson wrote to Mrs. Hahn on December 8, 1916, the day after he had paid a visit to Elyria, almost exactly four years after the strategic trauma, contained this sentence. "The experience ended in a convulsion that touched the edge of insanity." This letter helped convince Mrs. Anderson that the amnesia attack was real, and she authorized the use of the letter, which is extremely important to the probing of Anderson's psychology.

It seems unnecessary to describe in detail the content of the letters in this essay. However, I have prepared an index that contains references to well over 500 separate topics. Topics which have unusual numbers of references include the following: Advertising (28), Anderson Family Members (145), Art (44), Beauty (48), Chicago (133), Children (30), Courage (20), Criticism (21), Death (25), Escape (13), Financial Assistance (19), Freedom (17), Friendship (39), God (16), Illness (43), Imagination (16), Indianapolis (44), Industrialism (18), Isolation (21), Kentucky (17), Laughter (21), Loneliness (13), Love (97), Marion, Va. (33), Marriage (17), Nature (27), New Orleans (47), New York (54), Novels (28), Painting (24), Palos Park, Ill. (27), Paul Rosenfeld (17),

Stories (14), Strength (18), Swimming (12), Troutdale, Va. (37), Ugliness (16), Understanding (15), Vulgarity (12), Walking (28), War (15), Weariness (10), Women (72), Work (59), Writing (122), Youth (20).

Only one reference to a subject may often be most enlightening. There are literally hundreds of examples of that in the body of information and some misinformation in the Hahn letters. The topic-incidence list just given suggests strategic aspects of Anderson study and gives insight into the riches contained in the comments Anderson made to his special friend.

She was indeed a special friend. She doubtless loved him and would have been pleased to marry him. Although that possibility did not occur, she provided him with his most important single correspondence outlet, with the exception of Eleanor Copenhaver Anderson. (Anderson once accurately defined his personal correspondence as a way of expressing himself when he was solitary and thus as a record of his feelings in the absence of someone to whom to express them orally.)

Not only was Mrs. Hahn deeply interested in him personally; but she believed in his work, and she thought it most important that he have freedom to develop the artistic talent in which she believed. For approximately eight years (1921–1929, as well as can be determined) she contributed $100 a month to Cornelia Lane Anderson to help support Anderson's children, her idea being thus to give him freedom from the necessity of working to support them. When he had a chance to go to Europe with Paul Rosenfeld in 1921, she bought two of his paintings for $200 each to give him some money to spend. The matter of her financial assistance is mentioned in nineteen separate places in the letters. She visited Cornelia Lane Anderson's home in Michigan City, Indiana, and once stayed there overnight; she knew Tennessee Mitchell and appreciated her. She and her husband visited the Anderson rural residence, Ripshin, near Troutdale, Virginia, in August 1938. She had friendships with all three children, especially Robert Lane Anderson, but John Sherwood Anderson, the second son, said he did not know of any financial assistance by Bab until he read the letters.

The letters (only two by Bab have survived) are a record of a remarkable relationship between two remarkable people, one internationally famous, the other known only to a small circle of friends (and who, before her death in 1968, thought her name should not be related to the letters). She is mentioned as one of two persons (as M.D.F.) to whom Anderson dedicated *Sherwood Anderson's Notebook*. The other person was John Emerson, his lifetime friend from Clyde.

Mrs. Hahn had autographed copies of all his books but one. Her boxed copy of a special edition of *Sherwood Anderson's Notebook,* limited to 225 numbered and signed copies, 210 of which were for sale, has "author's copy" written in beside "This copy is No." Below is the signature "Sherwood Anderson." Moreover, the fly leaf has "To/Marietta Finley/With Love/Sherwood Anderson." Mrs. Hahn was kind enough to add on that page the following note when she made a present of the book to me: "To William A. Sutton-/ from the 'M.D.F.' to whom/this book was dedicated/along with John Emerson-/Best wishes for the success/of the new literary project/-Marietta F. Hahn-/1962."

The "literary project" she was referring to was *The Road to Winesburg,* which was published in 1972. She was also perfectly willing to have the letters published. However, because the selection of Anderson letters published in 1953 did not sell well, publishers were not interested. Finally, in February 1972, Dr. Richard E. Langford, president of Everett Edwards, Inc., professor of English at Stetson University, De Land, Florida, and one who had long had admiration for Anderson's work, gave me oral assurance of his willingness to publish the letters, having only conversational knowledge of them. It took until December 1972 to get the agreement of Eleanor Anderson, who at first declined permission, to allow publication. A contract for permission was finally prepared in late January 1975.

The letters, the texts of which I have prepared and annotated, are now available to play their role in the continuing study of the life and work of Sherwood Anderson. The title of the collection was inevitably suggested by Sherwood's customary salutation: *Dear Bab: Letters of Sherwood Anderson to a Friend.*

Anderson and Myth

DAVID D. ANDERSON

I

In August 1924 Sherwood Anderson had just finished reading the proofs of *A Story Teller's Story* and, writing to his brother Karl about that volume of what was for him autobiography, he said, "Don't know about *A Story Teller's Story,* whether I got what I went after or not. I didn't try to set down obvious facts, only tried to get the spirit of something."[1]

The statement was not only curiously prophetic of much of the adverse criticism directed at the work when it appeared and since—the common core of that criticism is that the work is formless and that it treats facts casually—when, indeed, it recognizes them at all—but at the same time it was as close as Anderson ever came, in any of the many statements he made on the nature of fiction and the process of writing, to indicating what it was that he had attempted in each of his works. From the early, destroyed "Why I Am A Socialist"[2] to *Home Town* (1940), the last work he published in his lifetime, and the posthumous, twice-edited *Memoirs* (1942, 1969), Anderson was concerned not with facts or with things but with whatever it was, often only vaguely defined, that gave them purpose and meaning.

That brief comment to his brother, significant in a time of Anderson's life when, as he approached fifty, he was attempting desperately, almost feverishly, to understand himself, his life, his time, his relationships with his past, his father, his place and his craft, in many ways describes the search, both literary and personal, that he had begun more than a decade before and was to carry on until his death nearly twenty years later. Anderson's search, as he had suddenly realized at that vital point in his career, was for "the spirit of something," for the beauty of the reality that lies beyond the facts; consequently, "I have perhaps lied now and then . . . ," he wrote in *A Story Teller's Story*, "but have not lied about the essence. . . . In the world of fancy . . . no man is ugly. Man is ugly in fact only. . . . It is my aim to be true to the essence of things . . ."[3]

The tangible result of Anderson's search of more than thirty years is the body of his work: some of the finest short stories in English or any other language, and an impressive array of other works that are less than his best but, much contemporary and recent criticism notwithstanding, none of them a failure. That body of work, that impressive documentary record of Anderson's search for the essence of things, for the beauty that lies beyond human experience, is expressed in what Northrup Frye calls "the only possible language of concern,"[4] a language that, for Frye, is called *myth;* for Anderson, "the spirit of something." In neither case are facts important; just as Anderson admitted frankly and guiltlessly that he lied, Frye, on a more sophisticated level described myth as having "more to do with vision and with an imaginative response than with the kind of belief that is based on evidence and sense experience."[5]

Whatever distinctions may be drawn between the admission of the artist and the definition of the critic are far less consequential than the shortsightedness of so many of Anderson's critics, then and more recently, who failed to see the unity and the beauty that lie beyond what has been called garbled history or garbled autobiography. The first is an early definition of myth,[6] and the latter is the essence of Irving Howe's insistence that *A Story Teller's Story* was "neither record nor fiction, loyal neither to fact nor to imagination,"[7] a statement that unfortunately misled too many of Howe's contemporaries and followers and caused them to ignore a book central to Anderson's work, his craft, and his life.

Howe also points out that Anderson was not one of America's "willful mythmakers,"[8] and it is certainly obvious that he was not one of those who constructed or perpetuated the images of America popular with the followers of Horatio Alger, Jr., or Russell Conwell. Anderson had spent too many of his days "in the writing of advertisements for somebody's canned tomatoes"[9] to become, consciously or not, a booster, one who would "pile up words to confuse"[10] or to mislead. For Anderson, essence, not appearance, was reality; nevertheless, in attempting to define that essence, clearly and in detail, he became, consistently and eloquently, one of the compelling seekers of the American reality, one of its most dedicated interpreters, and one of the most dedicated and reverent makers of the American—indeed, the human—myth.

The recognition that Anderson was a mythmaker is not new; James Schevill wrestled tentatively with the idea in his biography in 1951,[11] as I did, more reluctantly, in my own study sixteen years later,[12] and more recently Benjamin Spencer has examined Anderson as "American Mythopoeist" in a moving essay in *American Literature.*[13] What is new, and what I intend to explore here, are the dimensions of his mythmaking and the deliberateness with which he defined and observed those dimensions, two vital aspects of the attempt to understand a literary artist, the goal of whose art and craft was the delineation of what he called the essence of things.

Central to this consideration of Anderson the delineator of the essence of things and Anderson the mythmaker is his own concept of the complex relationships among Sherwood Anderson, average American male, "a rather heavy-looking individual going along wearing a suit of clothes, socks, shoes, any amount of gent's furnishings";[14] Sherwood Anderson, storyteller, who "spends most of his time trying to get out of his system certain stories";[15] Sherwood Anderson, romantic wanderer, seeking to tap the roots of the American experience—his own, that of his father, and that of "that strange, grotesque, sweet man,"[16] Abraham Lincoln; Sherwood Anderson, townsman, possessed of the conviction that "we Ohio men have taken as lovely a land as ever lay outdoors and that we have, in our towns and cities, put the old stamp of ourselves on it for keeps";[17] and Sherwood Anderson, writer and former businessman, fascinated with his own escape from business, motivated by a belief that beyond escape one may find fulfillment, and convinced that his own story, his experience, reduced to its essence and then disseminated widely in whatever form that essence demands, might yet become the American story and ultimately the essence of the American experience.

Anderson the craftsman and Anderson the storyteller share with Walt Whitman a peculiar self-identity: that of the average man who, like Emerson's poet, is one with his fellows but whose eye is keener and intuition more sensitive and who consequently, at whatever cost, permits those of us who are not so gifted to see with his eyes beyond the immediate to whatever lies beyond. Thus, Anderson, with confidence in the face of increasing adverse criticism, proclaimed as early as the winter of 1923–24 that he was writing, in *A Story Teller's Story* and, by implication, in the canon of his works, "an autobiography of a man's fanciful life. In that," he insisted, "I have been more interested than in any account of facts."[18]

In Anderson's search for the "spirit of something," "the essence," the central incident in both his factual and his fanciful life was his decision, at age thirty-six, to leave his moderately successful business career, to earn his living in whatever undemanding way he could, and to pursue a career as a writer of fiction. These incidents, taking place over several months during the winter of 1912–13, have been recounted a number of times by Anderson's biographers as a series of confusing and intriguing but relatively uncomplicated events; they have also been used as the basis of much of Anderson's fiction, most notably *Windy McPherson's Son,* his first published novel; *Poor White,* his best novel; and the two novels that follow, *Many Marriages* and *Dark Laughter.* They are also the first manifestation of the fundamental myth that Anderson created, the myth of escape and fulfillment, a myth that dominated much of his work over nearly all of his literary career.

This myth as Anderson created it appears in three forms: that in the early fiction, roughly to 1923; that which appears in his accounts of "a man's fanciful life" in the autobiographical volumes written in the mid-1920s; and that which dominates both fiction and nonfiction during the last fifteen years of his life. The earlier form is both simpler and easier for his critics to understand or accept; the second has been almost uniformly overlooked; and the latter, in several forms, has become the most profound and most durable.

In *Windy McPherson's Son* the myth appears for the first time. In four phases, it carries the protagonist, Sam McPherson, through ambition, rejection, search, and fulfillment, a formula much more closely related to that developed by the great romantic poets of the nineteenth century than to the work of Anderson's contemporaries. It is also closely related to the faith that took generations of people from Europe to America, from the East to the West, and finally from the country to the city, a migration in which Anderson himself had participated.

The parallels between Sam's life and Anderson's own—the central image of the father, the role of the mother, the preoccupation with success, the nature of the town and the city— are more significant in many ways than the plot, but that plot was Anderson's first attempt to define the essence of what he believed had happened to him and to America as the pursuit of happiness became corrupted by the promise of material success. At the same time the plot suggests the ease with which he apparently hoped or perhaps even believed that a new, spiritual, and humane fulfillment might be found, a suggestion that, in the last Elyria and early Chicago years, those in which he wrote the novel, Anderson must have known was misleading if not downright fraudulent when accepted literally.

In spite of the fact that he recognized the weakness of the novel's optimistic conclusion—he rewrote the ending, with no more conclusiveness for the second, 1922 edition—he continued to permit the myth of rejection, of escape to fulfillment, to dominate his fiction. In *Marching Men* he depicts a bitter, headlong assault on the same perverted values that had misled Sam McPherson. The assault is both literal and metaphorical and, like Sam's rise to success, it is ultimately unsatisfactory. At the end Anderson took refuge in ambiguous oversimplification as the novel's protagonist, Beaut McGregor, and his wife deliberately chose the path composed of continued resistance, a threatened ultimate failure, and a promised personal fulfillment together.

Even *Winesburg, Ohio,* a major stylistic and structural advance over the first two novels, contains suggestions, however muted, of the same ambiguous promise: as George Willard, in the final sketch, "Departure," leaves the town, his apprenticeship served and his goal a vague success in the city, he goes West, not, however, to follow the setting sun, but to conquer Chicago; Winesburg (or Clyde or Elyria) had become for George not a source of satisfaction or fulfillment, frustration or oppression, but "a background upon which to paint the dreams of his manhood."[19] In its ambiguity the ending approaches a Twain-like purity, but at the same time it adds a further dimension to the myth, the dimension that had led George Willard, Sherwood Anderson, and hundreds of thousands of others to Chicago, among them Sister Carrie and Theodore Dreiser, Felix Foy and Floyd Dell, all from small Midwestern towns; later, it took Upton Sinclair's Jurgis from Lithuania; and still later, Bigger Thomas and Richard Wright from the black South. Each, whether creator or created, went confidently to a success that ultimately proved elusive or nonexistent.

Yet recognition, search, and success continued to be the fictional reality for Anderson, most notably in *Poor White, Many Marriages,* and *Dark Laughter,* the latter the last of his novels of escape. But in each of them Anderson's honesty and grasp of reality prevail; in each, a note of mockery is directed at those who find an easy fulfillment or, perhaps more accurately, believe that they have found it and move confidently to accept it. At the end of *Poor White,* as Hugh McVey and his wife move toward each other in acceptance and understanding, the factories whistle triumphantly, and what is left is ambiguous at best; at the conclusion of *Many Marriages,* John Webster remains trapped, his long explanation misunderstood (as it has been by Anderson's critics) and the woman at his side a stranger; and in *Dark Laughter,* as Bruce Dudley, the refugee from artistic liberation, elopes with his new-found love, the blacks laugh mockingly and wisely as they recognize the futility of escape.

II

This, then, was the early nature of the myth Anderson created, a myth essentially romantic and yet real, based upon his own concept of what had happened to him and what might yet happen to America and Americans; this is also the myth that he gave widespread dissemination for the first time under the prosaic title "When I Left Business For Literature" in *Century* for August 1924, and a short time later, in identical words, in *A Story Teller's Story;*[20] at the same time it is the story of the beginning of his search for "the spirit

124

of something," for the meaning of his own life and for his own identity in the context of the time and place that had given him purpose and direction.

As Anderson's biographers and critics have pointed out on many occasions and for many reasons, his accounts of his departure from his business career are pure fiction, accounts that are at once rational and mystic, contrived and intuitive. In terms reminiscent of the long explanation that occupies much of *Many Marriages,* Anderson describes the incident first of all as a moment of insight into himself and his father simultaneously:

> It came with a rush, the feeling that I must quit buying and selling, the overwhelming feeling of uncleanliness. It was in my whole nature a tale-teller. My father had been one, and his not knowing had destroyed him. The tale-teller cannot bother with buying and selling. To do so will destroy him . . .[21]

From this moment came the first impulse to escape:

> There was a door leading out from my office to the street. How many steps to the door? I counted them, "five, six, seven." "Suppose," I asked myself, "I could take those five, six, seven steps to the door, pass out at the door, go along that railroad track out there, disappear into the far horizon beyond. Where was I to go? . . . I was still respected in the town, my word was still good at the bank. I was a respectable man.[22]

To Anderson, in retrospect a decade later, this moment was no less than a microcosm of the American experience:

> The American is still a wanderer. . . . All of our cities are built temporarily. . . . We are on the way—toward what?

... the American man has only gone in for moneymaking on a large scale to quiet his own restlessness . . . there is no time for unquiet thoughts.

On that day in the office at my factory I looked at myself and laughed. The whole struggle I am trying to describe, and that I am confident will be closer to the understanding of most Americans than anything else I have written, was accompanied by a kind of mocking laughter at myself and my own seriousness about it all . . .

. . . Any American will understand that.[23]

After his moment of insight, of his discovery of his own identity as a craftsman and as his father's son, of his recognition that his experience, in microcosm, was the American experience of his time, the rest of the account of the incident, that about which so much has been made in Anderson biography and criticism, that which became the foundation of what has been called the Anderson myth, is actually anticlimax in spite of its dramatic quality. First, Anderson records what is ostensibly an awareness that he must make a rational explanation to his secretary, to whom he had stopped dictating in the middle of a typical business-English sentence:

... Could I explain it all to her? The words of a fancied explanation marched through my mind.

"My dear young woman, it is all very silly, but I have decided no longer to concern myself with this buying and selling. It may be all right for others, but for me it is poison. There is this factory. You may have it, if it pleases you. It is of little value, I dare say. Perhaps it is money ahead, and then again it may well be it is money behind. I am uncertain about it all and now I am going away. Now, at this moment, with the letter I have been dictating, with the very sentence you have been writing left unfinished, I am going out that door and never come back. What am I going to do? Well, now, that I don't know. I am going to wander about. I am going to sit with people, listen to words, tell tales of people, what they are thinking, what they are feeling. The devil! it may even be I am going forth in search of myself."[24]

So thoroughly imbued with the enchantment of that vision of his own personal escape did Anderson remain that five years after having left Elyria and the paint factory—five years of writing advertisements in Chicago as well as publishing two novels, a book of verse, and many of the stories that were to become *Winesburg, Ohio*—he still envisioned a future that was free, as he made clear in a letter to Van Wyck Brooks:

> God damn it, Brooks, I wish my books would sell for one reason. I want to quit working for a living and go wander for five years in our towns . . .[25]

A short time later, just before the success of *Winesburg, Ohio*, he wrote to Trigant Burrow in the same vein:

> . . . I hate to see the years and the days go by in the writing of advertisements for somebody's canned tomatoes or in long days of consulting with some fellow as to how he can sell his make of ready-made clothes instead of the other fellow. I want to go up and down the great valley here seeing the towns and the people and writing of [them] as I do not believe they have been written of.[26]

In spite of his remembered account of the event, the reality for Anderson in his office in Elyria, Ohio, in the late Fall of 1912 was not the promise of an escape into fulfillment, but it was the predicament of a middle-class family man, father of three children, the youngest only a year old, and it was the prospect—a prospect soon realized—of exchanging necessary enslavement in a business office in Elyria for necessary enslavement in an advertising office in Chicago. It was a prospect Anderson must have anticipated at the time, but as he recounted the escape a decade later, realization of another kind came to him at that moment:

> . . . There was wanted a justification of myself not to myself, but to the others. A crafty thought came. Was the thought crafty, or was I at the moment a little insane, a "nut," as every American so loves to say of every man who does something a little out of the groove . . .
>
> . . . What I did was to step very close to the woman and looking directly into her eyes, I laughed gaily. Others beside herself would, I knew, hear the words I was now speaking. I looked at my feet.
>
> "I have been wading in a long river, and my feet are wet," I said.
>
> Again I laughed as I walked lightly toward the door and out of a long and tangled phase of my life, out of the door of buying and selling, out of the door of affairs . . .
>
> . . . "My feet are cold, wet and heavy from long wading in a river. Now I shall go walk on dry land," I said, and as I passed out at the door a delicious thought came. "Oh, you tricky little words, you are my brothers. It is you, not myself, have lifted me over this threshold. It is you who have dared give me a hand. For the rest of my life I will be a servant to you," I whispered to myself, as I went along a spur of railroad track, over a bridge, out of a town, and out of that phase of my life.[27]

Nowhere in either account does Anderson suggest the series of incidents that followed—his disappearance and hospitalization in Cleveland, the inane accounts that appeared in the Elyria *Evening Telegram* and the Elyria *Democrat,*[28] as well as those in the Cleveland *Press* and the *Leader*[29] of his breakdown and his return to Elyria, the care with which he wound up his affairs, and the deliberateness of his determination to return to Chicago—once more to an advertising office as well as to a liberation movement and a writing career.His break with business was certainly not a literal break, although he implied clearly that it was.

But to Anderson the physical continuity was meaningless. The reality of the move, that which he had tried to make clear in his fiction as well as this allegedly factual account, had nothing to do with what he actually did. The real break was spiritual and allegorical; not only did he never again give a lasting allegiance to anything except his art and his craft, but at the same time his experience became for him the archetypical experience of the artist, of the American, of the human being in the twentieth century, who must consciously reject materialism if he is to survive and pursue his vision of happiness.

Although Anderson proclaimed to the end that he was a simple townsman, an observer and teller of tales—just before the final trip in March 1941, which ended with his death in a hospital in Panama, he explained that what he would like to do on that journey was to "get up into some South American town, say of five to ten thousand people. . . . as far as possible getting to understand a little their way of thinking and feeling, and trying to pick up the little comedies and tragedies of their lives . . . ,"[30]—it is evident that from his departure from Elyria to the end of his life his concern was for the spirit rather than the facts of what he learned in his search, that through his art and his craft the facts would then be transmitted into something a great deal more meaningful than they were in their natural, limited settings.

III

For the next seventeen years after publishing *A Story Teller's Story*—to the end of his life in the midst of that fateful journey—Anderson sought to define that essence, that spirit distilled from mere facts, and the result is a curious but significant unity in his work, a unity that he had intuitively pursued earlier but by 1924 had began consciously to seek. During these years Anderson's attempt to define the myth underlying his own life and his country's experience takes on a new emphasis, not upon escape and an easy fulfullment, but upon the reality of a search that may never end.

That search, a continuation of the search that had begun with his acceptance of the necessity for rejecting materialism, for revolting from modern industrial America, more than a decade before, takes, from the time he wrote *A Story Teller's Story,* a distinctly different turn. No longer the attempt to portray a symbolic escape, it is, simultaneously, the search for the meaning of his own experience, that of Sherwood Anderson, his father's son, literary craftsman and teller of stories, and the meaning of American experience in his time. An attempt at fusion, at defining a microcosmic relationship between himself and his America, it was, in essence, the attempt to find a truth higher and more profound than that of mere fact and to find and define the spirit beyond fact. He had indeed defined his purpose in writing his spiritual autobiography, but at the same time, it became clear to him that that purpose was also to be the substance of his work from that point on. It was evident to him that the ultimate truth was not the act of rebellion but the search that followed, and that search became for him the substance of the ultimate meaning and myth of America.

The first attempts to define that essence were a curious pair of works: *Dark Laughter,* the ambitious novel that was as close to a best-selling commercial success as Anderson ever wrote, and *The Modern Writer* (1925), a brief, limited edition statement of faith. *Dark Laughter,* a work which came easily for Anderson, a book which "flows like a real river,"[31] as he wrote to Paul Rosenfeld while writing it during "days [which] have joy in them,"[32] has stylistic shortcomings that result from his shortlived search for a modern idiom, but it is an important book—important in Anderson's work and important to Anderson himself. Equally important in a different dimension is *The Modern Writer,* Anderson's first attempt to define the nature of his craft.

A transitional work between Anderson's early visions of escape and his definitions of the essence of his experience,

Dark Laughter, is Anderson's fictional interpretation of the meaning—for him as well as for his time and place—of the Chicago Liberation, the movement that promised a fulfillment that it not only could not deliver but instead substituted for the old material enslavement a new kind of submission, a conformity as destructive of the individual as was the old materialism. To Anderson it had become clear that the revolution proclaimed by the Liberation was neither the answer to conformity nor the fulfillment sought; rebellion was but a beginning, an opportunity to construct a new, uncomplicated life, not among the sophisticates, those who seek freedom in a demeaning submission to values that, like those they protest, are extraneous and artificial, but among an uncomplicated, unpretentious people. The laughter of blacks in the background of the novel, the "dark laughter" of a natural freedom, stands in stark contrast to the factory whistles that echo throughout *Poor White;* while both are mocking, the whistles mark a mechanical superiority, but the laughter of the blacks is human, uncomplicated, simple, and close to the natural origins of life itself.

In effect, *Dark Laughter* is the rejection of rejection, the rejection of an easy answer to a complex search that had begun for Sherwood Anderson on the dusty main street of Clyde, Ohio, in the 1890s; for his father, Irwin, in his first visit South as an Ohio cavalryman thirty years before; and for Americans in general in the restless movement westward that carried them across an ocean and distributed them across a continent. For Anderson, for the first time, it was evident that rejection and rebellion were symptoms of a vision, a vision as subject to corruption as any other human endeavor, unless one was wary, and, with a clear idea of his origins, his identity, and his purpose, he was determined to be as wary in his work as the townsman on the midway at the county fair.

All this is evident in *The Modern Writer,* another microcosmic work. The "modern writer" he attempts to define is surely Sherwood Anderson, but it is also the archetypical

American, now, for the first time, sure of himself. Echoes of Walt Whitman abound in his assertion that the writer is but another workman, differing only in that he is a workman "whose materials are human lives";[33] his goals must be honesty, must be "control over the tools . . . and materials of his craft."[34] Of most importance, it is evident that Anderson had learned the nature of fulfillment, an ideal and a reality not fixed but in constant flux, the fulfillment of the craftsman who rejects the mass-produced for a demanding, organic work that is in itself both fulfillment and reward: "You are undertaking a task," he asserts, "that can never be finished. The longest life will be too short to ever really get you anywhere near what you want."[35]

To Anderson at this point work, identity, and purpose had become one, a mosaic, all of the pieces of which, however, he had not yet identified individually. But the totality of that mosaic was not merely his own life and work; it was clearly that of all the people of his time. For Anderson, as for Whitman and Emerson nearly a century before, it was evident that not only was life itself a continuous whole, but that beyond it lay truth. To Anderson, the writer's responsibility was to define that truth in work that laid bare, in increasing detail, the essence of experience. That essence, that "spirit of something," might never become entirely clear, even in several lifetimes, but the pursuit and partial delineation of it gave meaning and direction to life. Consequently, to Anderson, the craftsman, literary or other, shared, in perhaps a minor but never an insignificant way, in the creative process that has gone on from the beginning.

The fifteen years remaining in Anderson's life were years devoted to searching, examining, and attempting to gain understanding of himself, his time, and his experience as they reflected and were reflected in the world around him. His decision to locate himself permanently in western Virginia, to build the stone house at Ripshin Farm, to purchase and edit the town newspapers in Marion, are all reflected in the work that he produced during the rest of that decade.

132

In those writings between 1926 and 1930, he defines, in essence and in spirit, the experiences that had led him to self-discovery and to the discovery of the meaning of the American experience in his time. These works—*Tar: A Midwest Childhood* (1926), *Sherwood Anderson's Notebook* (1926), *A New Testament* (1927), *Hello Towns!* (1929), *Nearer the Grass Roots* (1929), *Alice and the Lost Novel* (1929), and *The American County Fair* (1930), the list a curious mixture of substantial, intense work and brief, limited, personal statements—are clear definitions of the spirit of the things that had affected him, shaped him, and directed him, the Americans of his generation and place in the Midwest, and those of a later generation in the South. In these works, clearly and for the first time, Anderson uses his own experience as the basis for an examination of the universal American experience of his time and our own.

The work of those years is rooted in simplicity—the simplicity of a Midwestern childhood and of small-town maturity—and in the conscious search for the spirit that gives that simplicity the dimensions of complexity and profundity. Of the works, *Tar* is the most important, the most effective, and the most durable, for at the same time that it explores the origins of the American experience, it creates a new dimension of the American myth and a myth of its own, that of the American childhood and the childhood of America, that of innocence and brutality combined and of the beginning of a search for a security and love that one knows in childhood and loses and tries forever to regain.

There is something of Freud in Anderson's delineation of the spirit of childhood, or perhaps, more properly, one may read something of Freud into it, but there is more of Emerson and even more of Whitman, who, like Anderson, saw in clearer detail and with deeper insight than most of their contemporaries. The attempt to recreate the growth of a boy "from the ages of consciousness and until adolescence begins,"[36] as Anderson comments on the jacket, *Tar* is also the record of the growth of human consciousness; it is, as he continues, "of course, autobiographical, as such a book would be bound to be, but it is not written as an autobiography."[37] As critics pointed out then and since, it defies an easy categorization.

As in *A Story Teller's Story,* Anderson is searching for the "spirit of something" that he had been seeking for so long. Consequently, some critics then and later insisted that he had lost whatever creative impulse he once had and was once again covering the same old ground, an unfortunate observation that has prevailed for too long, particularly because in a number of important ways *Tar* goes far beyond anything Anderson had attempted before in the search for origins of a myth that had misled him and his American contemporaries since the end of the Civil War.

In the book this myth is portrayed in ways quite different from those that influenced Sam McPherson in Anderson's first novel. McPherson was motivated by shame and by envy —shame for a father who was a failure in an age that worshiped success and envy for those who had learned to ride the crest of the times. As Sam's instinctive perceptions were focused by John Telfer, his vision was narrowed so that only success, a visible material success, had any significance. Nothing had any meaning except as an obstacle to be overcome or a tool to use in constructing a successful material reality.

However, *Tar* is neither a real nor an idealized portrait of a Midwest childhood, an America, or an era itself neither real nor idealized; it is an attempt to define the essence of simplicity, of innocence, and even of brutality, much as Anderson had defined these qualities in *Winesburg, Ohio.* However, at the end, Tar, the Midwestern child, is not moving out of that simplicity into an idealized, successful future, as was George Willard; instead he is hurrying into a twentieth century dedicated to hustling, to moneymaking, to the pursuit of a material ideal. The unthinking innocence, the omnipresent brutality, the simplicity itself are the very elements that not only permit the people of Winesburg, of the Midwestern

134

childhood, to move into the new age, but they make it inevitable that the people of that childhood do so. As Anderson concludes the book, he defined clearly what has been the foundation of the myth that had, in three hundred years, led America from East to West and from innocence to corruption, the myth that he had devoted his life and work to refuting and replacing:

> A boy, if he is any good, has to be tending up to his job. He has to get up and hustle. . . . What he had to do was to bring into the family all the money he could. Heaven knows, they would need it all. He has got to tend up to his job.
>
> These the thoughts in Tar Moorhead's head as he grabbed his bundle of newspapers and, wiping his eyes on the back of his hand, raced away up the street.
>
> Although he did not know it Tar was, at that very moment perhaps, racing away out of his childhood.[38]

At the end of *Winesburg, Ohio,* when George Willard boarded the train to move westward with the setting sun, westward to Chicago, the Mecca for thousands of Midwestern farm boys, he neither noticed that the train had moved on, and "the town of Winesburg had disappeared and his life there had become but a background on which to paint the dreams of his manhood,"[39] nor felt the impetus that motivated Tar—the specter of hunger and the glitter of success. Neither Tar nor George represent for Anderson either reality or idealization; they represent instead competing myths, those of the craftsman-artist and the successful moneymaker, myths that had come to a stormy confrontation in his own life, a conflict that he had finally, in middle age, been able to resolve.

That resolution is celebrated in *A New Testament,* enthusiastic if technically deficient verse prose, and in *Hello Towns!,* the product of his venture into rural journalism. In both, Anderson celebrates his newly accepted identity as artist-craftsman-townsman-editor, as well as one who had learned that his experience and the American experience had been one and would become so again. In *A New Testament,* he writes,

> I double my fists and strike the ground a sharp blow. Ridges of land squirt out through my fingers.
> I have remade the land of my fathers. I have come out of my house to remake the land.
> I have made a flat place with the palms of my hands.[40]

In *Hello Towns!,* designed to portray the life of the town as it passes through the year's cycle, the pulse of its life recorded in the pages of his papers, he writes again,

> Yesterday I drove my car down a street of our town I had never been on before. I did not know the street was there. Men hailed me. Women and children were sitting on doorsteps. "It is our editor."
> "Well, you have been a long time getting down here."
> When I drive on a country road in this county farmers or their wives call to me. "Come in and get some cider, a basket of grapes, some sweet corn for dinner." The women of the town and county keep the print shop fragrant with flowers.
> I have a place in this community. How difficult to feel that in the city.[41]

With the complexities of his own identity and those of his time and place firmly behind him, Anderson devoted his life to his work: the search for the "spirit of something" in works that define the continuing conflict that he had resolved but that America had not yet learned to understand. Thus his works alternate between exercises in celebration and myth-making at their purest—*The American County Fair, Alice and the Lost Novel, Nearer the Grass Roots, Death in the Woods* (1933), *No Swank* (1934), and, at the end of his life, *Home Town,* and the *Memoirs,* unfinished and twice edited

136

since his death—and the works that grew out of his recognition that materialism and industrialism had failed—*Perhaps Women* (1931), *Beyond Desire* (1932), *Puzzled America* (1935), *Kit Brandon* (1936), all mythmaking of another sort, statements of regret but at the same time of the human potential for a rediscovery of origins and renewal of values. At the heart of them is a new image, a new mythical hero or heroine who, Anderson was certain, would one day lead America out of its confused present and forward into its living past, the past of values still surviving, still strong in spite of the industrial-material complex whose weak foundations and inadequate framework had led to economic collapse.

This myth-image is a fusion of Anderson's past and his present; it is made of the mother who had dreamed her dreams for George Willard and had rubbed the chapped hands of Tar Moorhead, and of the women whose innocence, like that of Helen White, whose earthiness, like that of Louise Trunnion, and whose wisdom, like that of Clara Butterworth, fuse with the girls from the southern hills, the mill girls, the country girls, those who seek to use rather than to be used by the values and machinery that had already corrupted American men.

Anderson's first visions of this new myth-image—certainly not an earth-mother but a person of innate wisdom, strength, grace, and inner beauty—are in "Alice," the story of an East Tennessee mountain girl grown into a woman of the world, and in "Elizabethton, An Account of a Journey." In the former he defines the true beauty of a woman—that inner strength and love that permits her to give generously of herself and yet remain herself, and in the latter, after a tour of the mills, he observes the town's shoddy monument in the square and comments, "How I would have liked to see one of those delicately-featured, hard-bodied little mountain girls, done in stone by some real artist standing up there."[42]

The image recurs, expanded and fully fleshed, as Doris Hoffman in *Beyond Desire,* as the central figure in *Kit Bran-*

don, as the old woman of the title story that opens the collection *Death in the Woods* and in the young girl in "Brother Death," the story that closes it. She is the composite of the women of whom Anderson might have been thinking, as he wrote, in one of the last letters he wrote before embarking for South America and death,

> ... I have been very fortunate. A surprising number of very great people I have known have been women, not young, inexperienced women, but women who have been ground by life and fate into something very shining and beautiful.[43]

The chaos of materialism out of control, as vividly portrayed in *Beyond Desire* as in *Puzzled America,* has nevertheless the potential to become something different, something old and yet new, into which the innate strength that Anderson sees still existing in America—in women, but in men, too—might yet take us. This is the world that he portrays in *Home Town* and in portions of the *Memoirs,* a world symbolically rather than literally that of the small town, a world that prefers a simple, close—although far from perfect—way of life to that dominated by impersonality and greed.

This way of life was certainly that of the past, Anderson knew, and it was threatened in the towns where it could still be found. But at the same time it continued to survive, and, as Anderson made clear in his last major effort at defining the "spirit of something" in his *Memoirs* (much of which he wrote and thought of as "Rudolph's Book of Days," a far less prosaic title), it could be discovered, in space and time but also, most importantly, in one's self, if he were willing to pay the price of wandering, searching, and suffering, even of public ridicule, that that discovery demanded.

IV

Shortly after Anderson's death on March 8, 1941, Burgess Meredith introduced a radio drama presented by the Free Company, founded by Anderson and others earlier that year. The drama, "Above Suspicion," was to have been written by Sherwood Anderson, but it was unfinished at his death. In his introductory comments, Meredith said,

> . . . For thirty years Sherwood Anderson represented a vital part of the United States, the America of the small town. He was never fooled about our small town life; he saw its ugliness and pettiness and limitations, but he was never fooled about its good side either. He saw its beauty too; its courage and its never ending struggle for a freer life. Not only in his work did Anderson stand for freedom, he stood for it in his life. He was kind and gentle, he was the easy-going friendly American with everybody he met. But there was nothing soft about this friendliness. When it came to justice for the oppressed, to freedom for all in equal measure, nothing could move him. He was poor, he was not always well, but he was always ready to give himself for a juster, a fairer, a more honest world.[44]

Meredith might have added, and we surely must, that the essence of Anderson's dedication to human freedom, the goal of his personal search and that of the people about whom he wrote with wisdom and compassion, was that freedom about which Meredith spoke. And he might have added, as we surely must, that the "spirit of something" that Anderson defined so clearly, that which emerged from his own history and that of his time, is, as myth must be, the substance of concern—for himself, for the people in his life, and for those about whom he wrote. Anderson's mythical world, complex and yet simple, clear and yet profound, is the story, to paraphrase Northrup Frye, of the origin, the situation, and the destiny of the America of which Anderson was so intrinsically a part. And, if we continue to muddle through, to avoid a self-destruction either nuclear or narcotic, we may yet discover, as did Sherwood Anderson, the "spirit of something," that is, the reality that we have sought for the two hundred years since America became a nation and throughout the century in which Anderson lived and the continuing life of his work. And as long as that search goes on, the search, as Anderson well knew, that is the substance of human life, Anderson's works will be read and their meaning and significance will be clear and relevant. Myth and reality, fused and clearly defined, the essence of meaning in human life and the substance of Anderson's works, are the substance, too, of a literary reputation more secure than ever before as we observe the passage of a century since his birth.

NOTES

1. Anderson, *Letters,* edited by Jones and Rideout, p. 129.
2. Knowledge of this book depends on Anderson's testimony and Cornelia Anderson's memory. See Sherwood Anderson, *Memoirs* (New York: Harcourt, Brace, 1942), p. 186, and Sutton, *The Road to Winesburg,* p. 373.
3. Sherwood Anderson, *A Story Teller's Story* (New York: B. W. Huebsch, Inc., 1924), pp. 383, 78, 100.
4. Northrup Frye, "Literature and Myth," in James Thorpe, ed., *Relations of Literary Study* (New York: Modern Language Association of America, 1967), p. 40.
5. Ibid.
6. Lord Raglan, "Myth and Ritual," in Thomas A. Sebeok, ed., *Myth: A Symposium* (Bloomington: Indiana University Press, 1974), p. 122.
7. Irving Howe, *Sherwood Anderson* (London: Methuen & Co. Ltd., 1951), p. 143.
8. Ibid., p. 250.
9. *Letters,* p. 45.
10. Sherwood Anderson, "My Word to You," in United Factories Company catalogue for Oct. 1906, p. 5.
11. See James Schevill, *Sherwood Anderson: His Life and Work* (Denver: University of Denver Press, 1951), pp. 101–108, 348–51.
12. See David D. Anderson, *Sherwood Anderson,* pp. 163–73.
13. Benjamin Spencer, "Sherwood Anderson: American Mythopoeist," *American Literature* 41 (Mar. 1969): 1–18.
14. Sherwood Anderson in "Among Our Contributors," *The Century Magazine* 108 (Aug. 1924): n.p.
15. Ibid.

16. *Letters,* p. 121.

17. *Sherwood Anderson's Notebook,* p. 91.

18. "Among Our Contributors," n.p.

19. Sherwood Anderson, *Winesburg, Ohio* (New York: B. W. Huebsch, 1919), p. 303.

20. The account appears on pp. 489–96 in *the Century* CVIII, and on pp. 298–313 in *A Story Teller's Story.*

21. *A Story Teller's Story,* p. 308; *The Century,* p. 494.

22. *A Story Teller's Story,* p. 304; *The Century,* p. 494.

23. *A Story Teller's Story,* pp. 309–10; *The Century,* pp. 494–95.

24. *A Story Teller's Story,* p. 311; *The Century,* p. 465.

25. *Letters,* p. 31.

26. Ibid., p. 45.

27. *A Story Teller's Story,* pp. 312–13; *The Century,* pp. 495–96.

28. The Elyria *Evening Telegram,* Dec. 2, 1912, p. 1; Ibid., Dec. 3, 1912, p. 1; the Elyria *Democrat,* Dec. 26, 1912, p. 5; ibid., Feb. 6, 1913, p. 5; Ibid., Feb. 13, 1913, p. 8.

29. The Cleveland *Press,* Dec. 2, 1912, p. 2; the Cleveland *Leader,* undated (Dec. 3, 1912?) clipping in the Sherwood Anderson Collection, Newberry Library.

30. *Letters,* p. 465.

31. Ibid., p. 130.

32. Ibid.

33. Sherwood Anderson, *The Modern Writer* (San Francisco: Gelber, Lilienthal, Inc., 1925), p. 29.

34. Ibid., pp. 31–32.

35. Ibid., p. 44.

36. On the jacket of the Bonibooks edition.

37. Ibid.

38. Sherwood Anderson, *Tar: A Midwest Childhood* (New York: Boni and Liveright, 1926), pp. 345–46.

39. *Winesburg, Ohio,* p. 303.

40. Sherwood Anderson, *A New Testament* (New York: Boni and Liveright, 1927), p. 39.

41. Sherwood Anderson, *Hello Towns!* (New York: Horace Liveright, 1929), pp. 335–36.

42. Sherwood Anderson, *Nearer the Grass Roots* (San Francisco: The Westgate Press, 1929), p. 35.

43. *Letters,* p. 467.

44. In *The Free Company presents,* James Boyd, compiler and chairman (New York: Dodd, Mead & Company, 1941), p. 270. Meredith served as narrator in each of the plays in the series.